Thirty Years in a
Turtleneck Sweater

Nick Warren

1 3 5 7 9 10 8 6 4 2

Copyright © 2005 Nick Warren

First published 2005 by Ebury Press,
An imprint of Random House,
20 Vauxhall Bridge Road, London SW1V 2SA

Random House Australia (Pty) Limited
20 Alfred Street, Milsons Point, Sydney,
New South Wales 2061, Australia

Random House New Zealand Limited
18 Poland Road, Glenfield, Auckland 10, New Zealand

Random House South Africa (Pty) Limited
Endulini, 5a Jubilee Road, Parktown 2193, South Africa

The Random House Group Limited Reg. No. 954009

www.randomhouse.co.uk

Printed and bound in Great Britain by Mackays of Chatham plc, Kent

A CIP catalogue record for this book is available from the British Library.

Cover designed by Keenan
Typeset by Dan Newman/Perfect Bound Ltd

ISBN 0 09190 390 4

For Leila

Who gave me the inspiration in the form of Amelia and Jack, and then the encouragement and the time to see it through.

Foreword

By the early 1970s the British building industry was in a state of war.

On the one side were members of the various unions, striving to increase membership and to force changes in wages and working conditions through collective bargaining and industrial action.

On the other side were the construction companies, organised into an employers' federation, striving to maintain and maximise profits. Though smaller in numbers, the employers had significant resources as well as powerful allies in government and the media.

In between these two camps were non-militant unionists, non-unionists and a largely conservative union leadership. It was here, in this middle ground, that the major battles were fought.

The employers had introduced what became known as 'lump labour'. Through this tactic non-union workers were enticed to work in dangerous conditions on an ad hoc basis with wage incentives that included lump sum payments from which National Insurance and income tax contributions were not deducted at source. Employers would often double, sometimes even treble the wages of such non-union labour – a practice that divided the workforce and undermined collective bargaining.

Hundreds of workers suffered permanent and even fatal accidents every year due to a lack of safety conditions in the drive for productivity on these sites. The unionists were fighting for the full implementation of statutory basic safety conditions on all sites, one pound an hour wages, and a thirty-eight-hour week.

North Wales was the least organised and least militant of all the regions and so the practice of lump labour was almost endemic. It was here that a small group of union activists responded by waging a campaign to kill the practice of lump labour and increase unionisation in an attempt to standardise wages and conditions for all. These 'flying pickets', as they became known, would travel around the region in buses, stating their case in open-site meetings, and their actions began to turn the tide against lump labour. It was, largely, a rank and file initiative and threatened the conservative union leadership almost as much as it unsettled the employers' schemes.

The construction companies appealed to Parliament, and the Conservative government of the day turned to criminal law (as opposed to labour law) to settle the issue of mass picketing once and for all.

The Building Workers' strike of 1972 was a national campaign. When my father, Des Warren, played his part in the assault on lump labour at sites around North Wales and Shrewsbury, he could not have known that British unionism was about to change for ever. He could not have known that he would be sent to prison for his political beliefs, and that he would suffer for these principles for the rest of his life.

This is a personal and anecdotal account of those times, from the shifting perspective of a small child in the shadow of a great man.

The Set-up

Last night my father came striding in through the door and pushed his way past me to the kitchen to cut himself a sandwich. I thought nothing of it until it struck me that I hadn't seen him up and on his feet like that for about ten years. And even then he wasn't showing the same swagger, the same sure sense of self.

The last time I saw my father on his feet was at the end of one of my flying visits home. He was being held up under the armpits with some effort by me and my younger brothers, Andy and Chris, as we posed for the Instamatic with fake jollity.

We stood outside his back kitchen door in Chester and he strained to lift his chin, his white hair ruffled by too much slumber in front of the telly. His belly sagged and his once-powerful frame was now weakened by years of neglect and physical attack. He was always a heavy man, strongly built, proud of his broad shoulders and his trim stomach. His hands were slender, too elegant for those of a steel-fixer, many said. But now those hands were frail and quaking.

Just before the shutter clicked I cracked a pedestrian joke to effect some change in his pained expression for the sake of posterity. It worked. He raised his bushy eyebrows, focused his clear blue eyes on the lens and muttered a cheerful curse in my direction. That was over ten years ago.

The last time I saw him was in 2001, when I repeated the long trip home from Johannesburg to Chester after an urgent phone call from Andy. From the observation room, I gazed at my father's ashen, stubbled face. He was asleep but clearly struggling to breathe. The bedclothes were in disarray, revealing bare, skinny legs. I went in, covered him up and sat in the plastic chair next to him, my eyes drawn, for some reason, to his feet. They were smooth and hairless, like white chocolate. They looked like those of a thirty-year-old swimming champion, not a battered ex-political activist in the latter stages of Parkinson's disease.

Leaning over, I greeted him with the forced and mischievous humour I knew he liked. His eyes sprang open and his lips cracked to reveal two complete rows of yellowed, encrusted teeth. They told me they couldn't clean his teeth because he couldn't swallow and might choke on the toothpaste.

His entire body was derelict, every muscle in that once magnificent frame atrophied to the point of meaninglessness: his bowels; his bladder; his tongue.

The nurses cheerfully told me that he was 'a cheeky bugger' and that he'd probably never stand again. He'd have to be manoeuvred from one sleeping position to another for the rest of what would probably be his short remaining life. They told me all this with the practised cheery detachment of a motor mechanic assessing an old classic. He was 65 years old.

I felt the redundancy of the borrowed digital camera in my pocket and knew that posterity would never be up to this lasting image.

I was staying at the Queen's Hotel opposite the train station, and met my brothers, Andy and Chris, there for a few beers. It was good to catch up with them after so many years.

We slid into an easy rhythm of conversation, fuelled by a selection of the local bitters. I raised some issues about how Dad was being looked after, and with the beer flowing it wasn't long before Andy started shouting that I didn't know what I was talking about, and I was well out of it. Chris kept his head down, waiting for a good moment to get another round in.

I sat at Dad's bedside in hospital for the first day and for another two days when he was returned to the one-bedroom flat that was his home.

He couldn't speak but he was looking at me and smiling, so I recounted stories from the past, events that dominated the landscape of my own childhood and well-worn anecdotes that brought choked belts of paralysed laughter from him – the colossal lead in most of these tales.

He stayed awake for most of what I said and smiled often, but I think he preferred the specially prepared photo album of my own small family back in the new South Africa.

During those three days he said just three things to me – one on each day: 'You aggravating bastard'; 'Two sugars, please'; and 'My teeth, clean my teeth!'

Parkinson's is a nervous disease that affects the muscles, and the final stages are frightening and protracted. For over twenty years, since my father became ill, I had thought only about the obvious muscles that move the body. I never considered those smaller, more self-effacing muscles which control the bowels, the bladder, the swallowing reflex, the lungs and the tongue.

So when my father strode through my home last night on his way to cut himself a sandwich, I was naturally taken aback. It was only midway through my spluttering speech of unfeigned joy and amazement that I had the most peculiar and regretful realisation: I was fast asleep, and my father was in a very different place, so far away.

A first memory

I'm standing outside the back kitchen door. I'm in shorts with no shoes. The cut grass is sharp, like Dad's whiskers when he doesn't shave. I can see patches of bird-poo and acorns from the old oak at the bottom of the garden. There's a warm grey concrete panelled wall on three sides of the garden to keep us safe from the neighbours and the alleyway where me and my mates have brick fights with the lads from the estate. There's sunshine everywhere, except in the spindly shadows of the oak. I'm dead happy.

It's like my face is open to the world with a grin I can feel in my whole body. I lean down and put my hands between my knees, like he tells me to. There's a thrill of fear and excitement because I don't know what he's going to do, but I trust him. He's standing behind me talking with his big voice but keeping it quiet. I can smell soap on his skin. I'm looking through my knees, salty with sweat, and I see his hands grab mine and then everything goes mad.

He pulls me topsy-turvy through the air and I watch the upside-down world right itself in a flash.

A blur of clear-lunged laughter and inexpressible joy falls from my mouth like the pollen that floats all round the garden.

Skeletons

I had two mums. One brought me into the world and left me to get on with it when I was six. The other mum came before I was seven and she looked after me for ages.

I remember my first mum like you remember bits of films from long ago: her getting dressed against the window in her bedroom so she looked like a shadow except for the brush running through her long, copper hair.

We lived on a council estate in Malpas Road, Ellesmere Port. The outside of the house was pebble-dashed and you could sit for hours picking off the tiny stones. Sometimes your hand would slip and you'd cut your knuckles and they'd bleed.

Dad was a steel-fixer. That meant he had to make steel skeletons before the concrete was poured to make foundations safe and strong. He used to work away a lot. When he worked closer to home he'd come back smelling of rusty steel and sit in his jeans and tell funny stories. He was young and powerful and handsome, and I thought he was fantastic. He was twenty-four when I was born.

Diane was born two years after me; Andy arrived two years after that.

When Dad was away at work in London or somewhere, Mum used to get visits from different men at night and we had to go to bed. When the uncles came round they'd give me presents. They probably gave presents to Diane and Andy as well but I can't remember. One uncle was a small, skinny man with nearly no hair on his head, and he gave me a tin piggy bank in the shape of a coffin, which you had to wind up. Then, when you put half a crown by the foot, a skeleton came up from the other end and this bony hand scraped the coin into the coffin where it rattled around. I'd play with it for ages up in our room under the covers so it didn't make a noise. Magically the coin was always gone by the morning.

That bald uncle must have been a bit of a favourite because he came round a lot. Sometimes I'd sneak down the stairs and sit halfway up, watching them through the banister. They'd be in the lounge, sitting on the sofa, drinking and talking quietly. Sometimes Mum would laugh. My eyes would burn because I was tired but I didn't care.

When Mum saw me, I'd say I couldn't sleep or something, and she'd drag me back up to bed and smack me hard and shout at me quietly so not to disturb the bald uncle downstairs. She used to smell of perfume with sweet breath from whatever she was drinking. Her face would be big and shiny against the light bulb in the ceiling when I looked up at her, and I wished she'd stay and shout at me and not go downstairs again.

Sometimes my nan would come to stay with us for a while and I'd sleep with her. That was good because there was someone to talk to. It put my mum in a bad mood though because no uncles came round when Nan was there.

Sometimes I'd get really thirsty and I'd get up and go downstairs and ask Mum for a glass of water. Nan would try and tell me not to bother her, but I would anyway and then Mum would thrash me all over the house, screaming because I'd gone too far.

Science

At the back of our house, down the alley and round the back there was a piece of wild common ground, not mowed like they did with the bit out by our front garden. Beyond this ground, far away, all pale blue and purple because of what the distance did when it passed through the air, you could see the refinery, its massive buildings with tall chimneys, steel tubes and pipes, and scaffolding for climbing. You could always smell the refinery even when the wind was blowing the other way – a thick, comforting stench like the whiff of an old broken car part.

I remember strolling down the alley with an empty plastic Corona lemonade bottle in my hand. My dad was home and he and Mum were shouting at each other and I was going to play in the little pond just out on the common ground. The summer was best because there were lots of insects swimming in the pond, and I would sit there for hours, inhaling the special smell that comes from poisoned ground.

Lying on my belly near the edge of the pond that day, I scooped up water alive with insects and frogspawn, and watched wispy threads of vegetation swirl like a thunderstorm in that tiny, secret underwater world. I dropped pebbles and bits of broken brick into the bottle, and saw them lollop down to settle on the bottom. I held the bottle back under the water and looked at the bubbles rising to burst on the surface. It was my own private world and I could do whatever I wanted with it.

I lay there for ages watching the smallest water insects in my lemonade bottle. Were they wondering what was happening to them? I didn't think it was cruel; it was just that one minute they were in a big pond, and the next in a bottle.

Buried all over that stretch of waste ground were pram

skeletons. Some of them even had wheels and then you could really go to town making go-carts with the older lads. But you had to be careful when you walked there because you could trip on bits of plastic bag and wire strands. But if I cut myself it was interesting because then I had a wound like the soldiers in World War Two against the Germans.

That summer day I kneeled down very slowly on a piece of broken glass till it broke through the skin. It didn't hurt all that much because my knees were tough. I smudged the blood to make it look worse than it was and walked home very carefully to show my dad. I wanted to make sure he could see the wound, but at the same time know that I wasn't going to moan about it. I was going to be brave. When I got home, I thought, my mum and dad would stop shouting at each other. Mum would clean my wound like a nurse and put a plaster on it, and my dad would say how brave I was but warn me about playing in dangerous places.

But when I got home Dad had gone and Mum just sent me up to my room.

Chewy

Our mum didn't like my younger sister, Diane. I did. She was lovely and looked ace when she was wearing blue. She had deep blue eyes and she used to smile and laugh a lot. It was a big, goofy smile and her laugh sounded like milk splashing on the pavement.

Diane was different from other kids because of something that happened when she was being born. She got stuck and didn't get enough air for ages, so she didn't grow up properly. She looked all right but she couldn't talk very well, so mostly what she did was laugh and then cry, even when she should have been too old to cry like that for so long.

One day we were walking round the estate when Diane saw a piece of chewing gum trodden into the path. She bent down and started peeling it off. It was a hot day and the soft chewy came off easy. Then she tried to eat it. She said she was hungry. I felt bad about this. I knew Mum thought she was just 'a greedy pig' but I was certain she shouldn't have to feel hungry so I went straight back home to the kitchen and stole some food for her. I can't remember what it was but it must have been better than flat old pavement chewy.

First school

My dad was at home for my first day at school, and he and Mum walked me down a long alleyway with a dark, strong-smelling wooden fence on either side. Dad said the smell was called bitumen and it was like tar. I thought it smelled like liquorice and later I licked a bit of the fence. It didn't taste like liquorice at all.

At the end of the alley were the school gates. They left me there and I had to walk across the playground on my own. I didn't want to go but my dad encouraged me. 'Go on, mate,' he said. 'You'll be all right.'

So I set off, trying to take big steps because I knew he'd be watching me.

The first boy I met was Terry; he lived opposite us and was my best friend for ages. He stopped me in the middle of the playground and he said, 'Are you a new boy?' and I said, 'Yes.' I don't know why I was a new boy; I can't remember why I wasn't there on the first day of school like everyone else but things were never really normal at our house.

We had little classes at that school. We did a lot of art. Christmas was the best time because it got dark dead early and the sky went purple; we had bits of coloured see-through paper on the windows and it was exciting in a way I can't describe.

The classes were quiet when we were doing art and you could use whatever colours you liked. I used to look at other people's pictures and see if they were better than mine – a lot of them were, but some of them weren't. Mostly we drew houses.

My dad used to make real houses for people to live in. He'd put steel in them so they'd be safe and would last for ages. You couldn't see the steel because they poured concrete all over it but Dad said that didn't matter – so long as it was in there.

Making pictures of houses was dead easy – a square with a triangular roof. The front of a house was like drawing a face, with two windows upstairs like eyes, a front door like a mouth with a path like a tongue leading from it to the pavement, and a gate with a fence if you were really good. On the roof you put a pointy-up oblong with smoke coming out of it, and that was it. You could do birds in the sky like stretched-out 'm's if you liked, and if you did a sun it had to have yellow strings coming off it. Grass was always green, and the sky always blue, but the house could be any colour you liked.

Sometimes the teacher would call me up to the desk to test my reading. I didn't like that because I couldn't read. It used to take me ages to get through a simple page of Peter and Jane. I read quietly so nobody could hear me except the teacher, and my face was always hot, my hands wet. But I liked Peter and Jane's pictures. They seemed really happy, had loads of things to play with, a mum that never shouted and a dad that was always there at the end of the day and at weekends.

Peter and Jane were about the same age as me and Diane, and they played together a lot. I used to play with Diane but it wasn't the same as with Peter and Jane because Jane could talk properly and she didn't laugh out loud all of a sudden at things I couldn't understand.

We used to get a third of a pint of milk every day at school. The milk was cold in the beginning, but if you took too long it'd get warm and a bit slimy and it wasn't so nice. Sometimes they'd deliver whole pints for the teachers to use in their tea in the staff room and if you were lucky you'd get the pint instead of the third.

Who got the extra pints and why was a mystery but I got one once. It's hard to drink a whole pint of milk when you're only six but I managed most of it. My dad used to sometimes go 'out for a pint' and I wanted to drink my pint too so I could be more like him.

Important questions

When the winter came it made all the grass and the mud hard with ice that hurt if you fell over. Jack Frost was a man who didn't live in a house and he'd come in the night and put frost everywhere and he really liked his job.

I came in from playing one day and asked Mum why my hands and knees were blotchy with red circles. She was sitting in front of the electric fire changing Andy's nappy and she said it was because I was handsome. Simple as that. (I felt good about my blotches after that, but they only came when it was cold. I thought the winter suited me best.)

Maybe because I felt handsome, or maybe because my mum had answered my first question and she seemed to be in a good mood, I asked her another question that was on my mind. I waited till she'd pinned Andy's fresh nappy, then I asked her what bollocks were. Her face went angry and she looked away from me and said in a hard voice: 'You know very well what they are!'

I didn't really know, but as soon as she spoke like that I did know what they were and wished I hadn't asked. It was as though I'd spoiled something.

Then Diane made it worse by starting to laugh and point at my face until Mum slapped her and made her cry instead. I got scared then and took Diane away from my mum as she pushed Andy into his cot and started rocking it too hard up and down, making the big springs screech and screech and screech.

Taking Diane upstairs to our room so we couldn't hear what was going on downstairs, I let her play with my toys till she stopped crying and started laughing again, and all the while under my breath I kept saying, 'Bollocks, bollocks, bollocks!' till it didn't mean anything any more.

The magic cupboard

I don't know what happened with my mum and dad but something must have made her leave when she did. They were never married and I suppose that made it easier for her to go.

The day my mum left us I was six years old. I was sick and off from school. I was lying on the sofa with a temperature. The sofa was made of horsehair, somebody said, and it was scratchy on your bare legs so you couldn't get comfortable and you'd have to twitch and keep moving.

She kissed me goodbye. I loved the way she smelled.

She told me that she was going shopping, and that there were toys and sweets in the magic cupboard.

The magic cupboard was a drinks cabinet in the lounge; you opened these two little doors and a light came on inside, throwing itself all over the mirrored walls, floor and ceiling. That light flew through the glass of the shelves and the tinkling glasses as though it was laughing.

The last memory I have of my mum is her closing the frosted glass of the door from the lounge to the hallway, then leaning down and picking up two suitcases in a broken silhouette. As soon as she closed the front door behind her I got up from under the blanket on the sofa and went to the window to see her climb into a taxi.

When the taxi drove away I went to the magic cupboard. Sure enough there were loads of toys and sweets to be had. I played with the toys and ate the sweets for a long time. It got dark long before Dad came home and I was scared. The house was warm because the fire had been on all day and I felt a bit sick.

When Dad came home he didn't even ask me where Mum

was because I suppose he knew. He had his big parka on and when he picked me up I could feel and smell the cold air he'd brought in with him. It made me feel better curling my legs around his hips as he walked round the house looking for things, not really knowing what to do.

He wrapped a blanket around Andy and carried him down the road with Diane and me following. At the telephone kiosk he called my nan and said some things that I didn't listen to on purpose. I just stood on the dirty concrete floor taking big smells of the kiosk. It smelled exactly the same as the lift in Nan and Grandad's flat. Outside I could see people walking against the wind and the whole world was dark, grey and sad.

Vandalism

That first Saturday with no mum, Terry and I went round to the school to mess about, see if we could nick anything, or maybe even break into school.

There was nothing to do so we got two crates of empty milk bottles and bowled them along the playground, watching them explode against the kerb where the teachers parked their cars.

We took bits of the broken glass and buried them in the sandpit of the school next door. I felt bad about this later because the school next door was for special kids and my sister Diane was one of them.

When Terry went home I walked back to the school but I didn't go in through the gates. Instead I sat on the edge of the pavement with my feet in the gutter as cars raced passed. I had a stick and I kept my head down and squashed a million red ants.

Dreadful thoughts of Diane running and laughing and jumping into the sandpit, cutting her skin open and bleeding. Wanting to go back there into the sandpit to find all the bits of broken glass but being too scared. What if someone caught me and I got into trouble? It seemed like everyone was in trouble those few days. My mum was in really big trouble because they said she wasn't coming back.

Gargantuan

I had three teddies, one was a fluffy teddy, a knitted floppy golliwog like on the Robertson's marmalade lids, and a hollow plastic teddy called Gargantuan.

My dad didn't like the golliwog because it had the word 'wog' in it and that was a bad word. My mum didn't care and she got me a badge made of steel with a golliwog on the front that she had to send away for. I used to wear it all the time except when Dad was home.

I loved Gargantuan because you could squash him in fights and he always just filled back up with air through the hole under his feet. I liked sucking and biting him because his skin was soft and smooth and tasted like the smell of milk.

One day I decided to give Gargantuan some tattoos. I took a blue pen and filled in all his grooves and the shaped bits around his eyes, nose and mouth, and his bubbled-up body bits.

As soon as I'd done it I wished I hadn't. He looked different. It was like I'd lost the real Gargantuan, like I'd sent him away and now he was someone different.

I tried to wash him with spit but it didn't work. It hurt my heart every time I looked at him after that and so I stopped playing with him and tried to forget where he was.

Sometimes I'd see him under my bed or in the toy chest and I'd look away and pretend he wasn't there.

Aunty Gill

Sprawled on the front seat for as long as I could stay awake, then sent to the back with Diane and Andy who are both asleep. Curling up in a brown scratchy blanket striped with reds and yellows. Fighting car fumes and trying not to sick up a belly full of biscuits and Shredded Wheat. The hum of the old Rover, with him solid at the wheel. Down that country lane in the nearly dark. Then, I hear a thump and from the corner of my eye I watch the back wheel overtake us on the inside and the car goes all wobbly.

'Hey, Dad – there's our wheel!'

Dad doesn't answer but instead he slows the car and yanks the handbrake through its ratchets. Then he gets out to fix the wheel back on to the car.

Stepping outside and watching him work. The black-green hedges scratch and murmur in the chill wind. 'Where are we going, Dad?' I ask. 'When will we be there?' I know something is over but I'm trying not to think about it. I take deep breaths but can't get enough air into my lungs until I think that whatever is going to happen my dad is going to be there with me so it'll be all right.

We pull up in a small narrow street on a hill outside my Aunty Gill's house in Bury. Aunty Gill opens the door as soon as she hears the car park, she runs outside and lifts me out of the car and squeezes me hard. It is fantastic and I never want her to let go. My dad carries Diane out of the back seat, Aunty Gill tells my cousin Tony to bring Andy and we all go into the house.

I had two older cousins. Tony was about ten and Jeff was about eight. They had sisters, too. Debbie was my age and Amanda was about four, like Diane. Everyone was dead pleased to see us and it felt good to be there, exciting in a way I couldn't really understand. Everyone was smiling and talking except Uncle Frank, a thin man with a mean face who kept quiet even when he took money off my dad 'for food and keep'.

Dad couldn't stay because he had to sort some things out at home but he'd pick us all up soon enough, he said. I didn't mind because Aunty Gill said she'd take good care of us in the meantime, and she did.

The pantry

When we got back to our house a week later everything seemed exactly the same, except our mum still wasn't there and Dad said she wasn't going to come back. It didn't make any sense to me and I asked loads of questions about where she'd gone and couldn't we go and get her, until he got fed up and said, 'Give it a rest, will you, Nicky?'

Dad had left his job far away and was working closer to home so he could look after us. He used to sit us in the pantry, the tiny room leading off the kitchen. There was nothing in there but shelves of food, a table, a few chairs for Dad and Diane and me, a food-spattered and crusty high chair for Andy, and a paraffin heater to keep us all warm. I loved the smell of that heater, because it made the small room a warm and cosy place.

Dad made porridge every morning when it was still dark outside and we had to eat it even if it was cold or had lumps in it.

Most nights, after school, after his work, we'd all sit round in the pantry and eat Dad's stew. He called it 'Superman stew' because I kicked up a fuss and didn't like it. Andy didn't like it either and so Dad did that trick with a spoonful coming all the way from the bowl, flying through the air to land in his mouth. It took him ages, but he didn't get bored.

Diane didn't need the Superman trick because she was too old, and anyway she never looked up from her bowl till all her food was gone and she wanted more.

The stew used to sit on the top of the paraffin heater to keep it warm, and through the high window you could look up and see the wide world outside at the beginning and the end of every day.

Living with just our dad was much better than living with just our mum because he wasn't as moody. I could ask him anything and he always gave me an answer. He never screamed or belted any of us.

Dare devils

School started up again. Me, Terry and some others used to go round to the other side of the estate where there was a high wall with a ditch and a little playground separating us from another estate.

The game was you had to stand with your back pressed to the wall and the others had to stand on top of the wall and wee over your head into the ditch.

The rules were you weren't allowed to move but you had to make sure the wee didn't get you. It was easy in the beginning because the wee went far out into the ditch, but when the weeing was nearly over it got weaker and it came closer and closer to you. If you didn't move it was your turn to get up on the wall and do the weeing. The thing was when you were doing the weeing to pretend you didn't mean to, but somehow wee on the other's head anyway.

It was late one afternoon when I saw a girl from the other estate in a bright yellow dress. She was nothing special really, just somebody's older sister, but in that yellow dress she looked fantastic. I somehow wanted to talk to her, to get close to her body, and maybe get her to hold me tight.

She was jumping from one big log to another. It was quite far, especially for a girl. In the middle of her jump her yellow dress flew up over her white belly. It was like slow motion. I found out later her name was Michelle, but there was no way I could ever talk to her.

I knew that girls grew faster than boys but stopped sooner, and decided that when I was as big as Michelle I was going to talk to her and make her like me and take care of me.

Drumnadrochit

It was half-term. Dad and me drove for a long, long time to get to Scotland.

I didn't know where or why we were going. Diane and Andy were back at Aunty Gill's but I didn't mind. I was with my dad and that was good enough for me.

We arrived at night in a small village on the edge of a big lake that Dad said was Loch Ness where the monster lived. There was snow all over the place, orange snow catching the light from the street lamps. It was late and I woke up when the car turned off, ticking as everything cooled down. It was dead quiet – that special quiet that comes after snow.

We walked across a patch of grass that was all white and

crunchy to get to the only house with the lights on in a row of little dark cottages. Dad held my hand and knocked on the door and we waited till it was opened by an old woman who didn't say anything but just let us in.

There was dark-brown patterned wallpaper, brown stairs and banister, and brown floors.

Dad introduced me to the old woman who said she was my nan. I knew she wasn't my nan because she didn't look like my nan and she didn't talk like my nan. I shied away from her and Dad explained that she was another nan. She was my mum's mum, and no, my mum wasn't here as well.

I didn't know what to say but I didn't want to be rude so I said hello and let her hold my hand.

There were two big boys there as well. Dad said they were my half-cousins but they looked very big to me.

They took me through to their bedroom. They told me they were my Scottish cousins and showed me their Airfix model Spitfires and bombers hanging in front of the little window by near-invisible threads of cotton.

It was strange. They were all nice and I wanted to like them but couldn't in case they wanted to keep me for ever. I didn't want to stay for ever. I was happy enough with my other nan, and my other cousins Tony and Jeff.

I tried hard not to cry, but every time they said or did something nice it became harder to breathe. I asked my dad if he was going to leave me there.

'No, mate, we're just visiting,' he said. 'I've got to sort some things out with your nan.'

That made everything a lot easier and after that I asked loads of questions about the Airfix model airplanes and didn't feel scared of my Scottish cousins any more.

Mum's the word

The only questions Dad wouldn't answer properly were questions about my mum. Whenever I asked him where she was or why she'd gone he'd tell me not to worry about it or 'never you mind' or 'I'll tell you later' – which he never did.

It made it even harder at school because the other kids knew my mum had gone away and they wanted to know where and why, and I couldn't tell them because I didn't know. Just talking about it made my stomach hurt and especially when they all said it must be rubbish to have no mum to look after you.

One of the bigger kids, Mike, said maybe she'd left because my dad was a communist and he wanted to kill the Queen, share out all our stuff and make us all work in factories. I didn't know what Mike was talking about and he told me he knew my dad was a communist because his dad had told him.

We got into one of those 'my dad's better than your dad' arguments and it ended with Mike saying that my dad couldn't even keep a wife so he must be crap.

I wished Tony and Jeff were there. They would have known what to say, but I didn't.

Tomatoes

Dad couldn't work near home for ever. Soon he had to take a job far away and he couldn't take us with him.

In the car again but this time Andy is with me. I don't know where Diane is. I'm thinking about what Mike said and I know my dad works on building sites and that he has fights with the bosses so they'll give him and his mates more money and keep them safe, but I don't know if that's the same as being a communist.

'Dad? Are you a communist?'

He laughs. 'I am, aye.'

I didn't want him to say that. I look out of the window. He's been through our cupboards at home and he's put a load of our clothes into a case. The case is in the boot. Communists can't keep their wives and I wonder if they can't keep their kids either. I don't want to think about it.

'Dad, do you want to kill the Queen?'

'I don't want to kill the Queen, but I wouldn't mind seeing the end of the monarchy.'

'What's the monarchy?'

'It's a blood-sucking institution made up of thieves and gobshites.'

I know it's not good if you don't like the Queen. Everybody's supposed to like the Queen.

'Dad, do you want everyone to share out everyone's stuff?'

'Only the rich bastards that have got more than they need but less than they want.'

I know lots of people don't like you sharing their things, especially if you're not going to give them back. I think maybe Dad tried to share some of Mum's things and that's why she left.

'Do you think we should all work in factories?'

'No, but everyone should have the right to work.'

We turn a corner and there is a big house on a hill, with a big garden rolling downwards and a hedge all along it.

We stop on the road and Dad brings out our bags and we went to meet the people who lived in the house.

They smiled a lot and spoke to my dad, then he moved towards the front door. I ran after him and grabbed his leg.

He laughed and ruffled my hair, but he wasn't laughing because I was being funny. 'I'll see you later, mate.'

'I want to come with you.'

'I won't be long.'

The people were foster-parents and they had lots of ornaments that we weren't allowed to touch. They told us that we could play in the garden but we mustn't touch the tomatoes at the bottom by the shed.

Me and Andy went down the garden to have a look. It was quite cold and my knees did that special thing with the blotchy skin and the sky was black and grey like oily steel and everything smelled thick and rich like when you squash an acorn. I felt sick in my stomach but Dad said he wouldn't be long so I thought I must just be hungry.

We found the tomatoes and they were growing on a bush. We'd never seen tomatoes on a bush before and wanted to know if they were real. Some of them were red like real tomatoes but some of them were green or orange. The green ones were hard but when we picked some of the red ones they were much nicer to eat.

Then the man came down and shouted, 'What did I tell you about the tomatoes!'

I hated the man for making Andy scared so I said, 'My dad's

a communist and he said the tomatoes are for everyone.'

He stared at me for a minute and his skin went white around his tight mouth. He said we had to go to bed.

Dad didn't see us later like he said he would and we had to stay in that house for ages with those people smiling at us and shouting at us not to touch the ornaments all the time.

Me and Andy used to stay up in our room for as long as possible so we wouldn't have to meet the people in the house except to eat and have our bath. We thought up ways to escape and go to Aunty Gill's house.

Every day I asked the people when my dad was going to come and get us and they'd say, 'Not soon enough!'

Railings

Later I wished I hadn't said anything because it wasn't my dad who came to pick us up but a stranger in a big coat and a small car that was too hot. She took me but left Andy behind.

Sitting in the front of the car, I didn't cry but trying not to meant that I couldn't talk properly either. She did that same thing that all grown-ups did, which was to be friendly and smile all the time, as if this was a great thing that was happening and I shouldn't worry.

Then she said we'd arrived and we got out of the car and she made a joke about how heavy my bag was and I was holding her hand and rattling my fingers along the railings of a long fence made of painted iron in a big quiet, tree-lined street, looking at my shoes fly over the pavement. It made me feel a bit dizzy.

The gates to the orphanage were like a gigantic ribcage. Beyond the gates was a long path leading left up to a building and right down to a big field where there were loads of kids and a playground with the usual swings, slide, roundabout and climbing frame.

The building was huge, too big for a house, but like a house with lots of windows – it didn't look like a face – and big steps coming down to the path that didn't look like a tongue.

After the lady introduced me to even more smiling grown-ups I spent a lot of time sitting on the steps watching the other kids playing in the playground. Then the lady put her hand on my shoulder and said, 'It won't be for ever and you'll like it here.' Then she went away.

Later a woman in a uniform with a smiling face leaned in close. 'Why don't you go and play with the other children?'

'I don't want to.'

But of course I did really. I was just worried that if I played with the other kids they might think I was happy and want to keep me there for ages.

At night I slept in a single bed in a big room they called a 'dormitory' with other kids. I had to sleep in my underpants because I'd lost my pyjamas and the other kids made fun of me so I pulled up the covers and pretended I couldn't hear.

Every morning, when I woke up, my bed was wet. I couldn't understand it, I was embarrassed, and I never knew how or when or why it happened.

They didn't like it and told me I had to stop doing it because

I was a big boy now. But there was nothing I could do about it. I didn't like it either. I think that's why they sent me home in the end.

Brazil

Dad had found work near Ellesmere Port. One day he came home with a sack full of Brazil nuts that he'd got from a mate who worked on the docks in Liverpool and he gave it to me. It was about half the size of a pillowcase and I took it straight outside. Taking out the musty nuts and smashing them open between two bricks and eating the insides till my teeth were thick with it.

Pretty soon kids from the estate came up and asked if they could have a Brazil nut. I handed them out one at a time and we'd smash them up and gulp them down. Before long there were kids all around me and even more started running over and we were all great mates and the nuts tasted ace and the whole thing was fantastic and it suddenly felt wonderful to be back home.

But when the bag was empty, everyone started strolling away to play their own games with their own friends again and I was left sniffing the sack. Running inside I asked Dad if there were any more Brazil nuts.

'No. That's your lot.'

'All my mates want some more nuts.'

'They're not your mates if they only play with you because you've got a big bag of Brazils. Off you pop.'

I knew there was no point going back outside with no more nuts so I just took the empty sack up to our bedroom and let Diane and Andy have sniffs of it.

Sooty and Sweep

Mostly I'd make my own way to school, but sometimes, if Dad wasn't working, he'd take me in the car. On the way he'd call in at the newsagent's to pick up the paper to see what was going on in the world.

Sooty and Sweep were two puppets on telly and they were brilliant. It wasn't that they were really funny or anything, it was more that they were on telly and they talked to kids. So one day, when Dad was taking me to school, and I saw a Sweep puppet on the front of a comic in the newsagents with the word 'free' next to it on a sticker, I got dead excited. 'Hey, Dad, look – can I have it?'

'Go on then.' Dad started taking the Sweep puppet off the front of the comic to give to me, but then the newsagent got angry.

'What do you think you're doing?' he said.

Maybe it was his tone of voice that got on Dad's nerves because he immediately kicked in. 'And who do you think you're talking to!'

The newsagent pointed at the comic in Dad's hand. 'You can't just take the puppet without buying the comic!'

'It says it's free, doesn't it?'

The newsagent started to come around to our side of the shop but when he tried to lift the counter to get through, Dad leaned down hard so the newsagent couldn't lift it and get out.

'It's free when you buy the comic! You've got to buy the comic to get the free puppet!'

The newsagent was panicking, but Dad was very calm.

'It doesn't say "free-with-the-comic", does it? It just says "free", so thanks very much, mate.'

The newsagent couldn't get out from his side of the counter so he started running up and down the narrow aisle on his side of the shop. 'I'll never be able to sell that comic without a free Sweep!'

Dad dug into his pocket with his other hand and put the money for his newspaper on the counter. 'Listen to yerself, you whingeing bleeder,' he said.

The newsagent looked at Dad's money on the counter and it looked as though he wasn't going to take it. But then he swooped on it like a bird and moved far away again.

'I know who you are!' he said. 'You're not welcome in my shop. I'll have the police on you!'

I pulled the puppet on to my hand and we walked out of the shop. At the doorway, I made Sweep look at the newsagent and in a squeaky voice, just like Sweep on the telly, said, 'Ta-ra!' Then I scurried out with my dad chuckling behind me.

At school everyone wanted to have a go with Sweep and he

lasted till lunchtime before our fingers wore through the flimsy plastic and he was in pieces.

Terry's old man

Some mornings I had to wait for ages after Dad had gone to work before I could take myself to school. I used to watch Dad going down the path to his car. If I stood on tiptoe, I could just about see over the window sill in the lounge.

Then I'd wait for the right shape on the clock on the cooker before I could go over the road and visit Terry. Most of the time they were still eating breakfast and sometimes Terry's mum would give me a little plate of what they were eating – beans on toast, sometimes with egg and bacon.

Terry's dad didn't like me; he'd make me stand outside in the doorway of the kitchen. It felt horrible not being liked. I tried to make him like me by saying things but it never worked: 'I had porridge for breakfast. It had lumps in.'

I would stand there for ages, watching the big vein on the side of Terry's dad's head as he chewed his food and stared at the pages of his newspaper. The smell of meaty grease hung in the air.

I didn't like Terry's dad but the funny thing was that Terry didn't like his dad either. I couldn't believe that somebody could not like their own dad, and it made me feel dead lucky because my dad was ace.

Fairground

Aunty Gill got rid of her husband, Uncle Frank, because he was 'no good' and she had to wait a while before she got married to Uncle Bernard who came from Manchester. But as soon as she did they moved from Bury to Blacon, which was nearer to Ellesmere Port and much easier for us kids to stay with them, and that was great.

When we weren't at home with Dad we were at Aunty Gill's and she promised me that no matter what happened we were never going to be sent away to people we didn't know ever again.

Sometimes the whole family would be there, our cousins Tony, Jeff, Debbie and Amanda, Aunty Kath and Uncle Ticker, Nan and Grandad, and it was fantastic to feel a part of the whole thing. Being with Aunty Gill was like being in the sunshine all the time and you just couldn't help feeling happy because she loved you.

When the house got too packed, me and Tony and Jeff would go out and play footy, or just wander round the estate. Tony and Jeff would show off new things they could do and I'd try to copy them, even though they were older than me. They had long hair and they used to do this thing where they'd snap their heads back suddenly and flick their fringes out of their eyes. I started doing that as well, but because I had short hair it didn't really do anything except make me look as though I had a twitch.

When we stayed there I'd get up in the mornings with all the others and I'd sit on the sofa watching Tony making a fire to warm the house. He'd lay the firelighters first, then bits of wood, then coal. Then he put the little coal shovel over the grate and a big piece of yesterday's newspaper over the shovel. Within seconds the fire would be roaring behind the paper. You could see the angry orange flames licking at the news headlines, and the fire would sort of howl trying to get out. A lot of the time the headlines were about the unions getting too strong, and I thought that was great because my dad was in the unions. Then, at exactly the right moment, when it was about to catch fire, Tony'd whip the newspaper away and the fire would quieten down and hide behind the pieces of coal, as though it was embarrassed.

'You can't trust fire, Nicky,' Tony would say. 'It's a bastard.'

Sometimes, when I hadn't seen my dad for a long time, I spent hours sitting staring at the fire just banging the back of my head against the back of the sofa.

Aunty Gill would sit next to me and pull me into her body and say, 'You all right, Nicky love?'

I said I was all right. Although I liked banging my head on the sofa I also liked it that she was worried about me so I did it a lot more that I really wanted to.

Dad used to introduce us to his new 'girlfriends' who were going to help look after us at our own house. They'd all lean over and put their big faces in front of mine and Andy's and Diane's, but you couldn't believe them – they weren't like Aunty Gill.

There was a fairground in Blacon and Dad came to visit us for the weekend and he brought this woman called Carol and we all went off to the fairground together. It was magic. There were loads of things to do and eat and ride.

There were these little aeroplanes and they were painted red and white and blue with two seats and short wings and they lifted up into the sky and razzed around in a circle high up there. I wanted to go on the ride with my dad, but Carol said she'd take me. I didn't want to go with her, but when Dad said I could only go if I went with Carol I said all right.

We were flying around up there and my mouth was crammed with laughs and screams. There were two big holes on each side of the dashboard in front of us and Carol opened hers and loads of air blew her hair all over the place. Then she reached over and opened the air hole on my side. I didn't like it because the air went straight into my mouth and I couldn't breathe properly. I asked her to close it; she told me not to be a baby and opened the air hole to full. I felt like I was going to die.

'Turn it off! I feel sick! I can't breathe!'

She just laughed and pushed my face closer to the air hole and then I was sick all over the place.

Carol was a nurse. I hated her.

It was dead late when we went home that night and the sky was black with no moon. All the street lights were on. After we parked the car I had to walk in front because of the smell of the sick on my neck and clothes. We all had coconuts and I knew from school that what you were supposed to do was open holes in two of the 'eyes', then you could drink the 'milk' that was inside. Dad kept saying that the coconut and me looked just like each other because of my short hair and Carol laughed. I tried to pretend I thought this was funny as well but it was hard because I didn't want to look like a coconut and I didn't like the way Carol was laughing at me and holding on to my dad's arm at the same time like he was hers and not mine.

We were walking down the pavement back to Aunty Gill's and Dad was holding her hand, making jokes and ignoring me, Andy and Diane. I kept walking back to him and pestering him to find out if he could open the coconut, then eventually Dad said, 'Give it here, I'll open it for you' and I thought, 'Ace.'

But he didn't open it nicely, instead he just took it off me and threw it high in the black sky where I couldn't see it, and then I heard it smash to pieces on the pavement ahead.

I ran as fast as I could but it was too late. All the milk was lying on the pavement like thick, white, nut-smelling blood. I couldn't understand why he had done it. They both walked past me, and Carol couldn't stop laughing.

I had to gather as many pieces as I could, then run to catch up with them before they went into the house and left me on my own.

Canal

As well as Terry I had another friend, Mark, who lived on the same road as me. His dad was a policeman. I was nervous about policemen because Dad was always going on about them being 'agents of the State'. I knew policemen were against communists and I was worried he'd find out about Dad wanting to share out the Queen's stuff to people who worked in factories.

Mark had a little brother like I had Andy, but Mark's little brother was weird – he used to 'kiss' earthworms.

'Go on – kiss a worm!'

'All right, I will.'

He'd purse his lips, kiss the worm then suck it into his mouth and swallow it. It was great to watch but it made you feel sick. If anyone asked you if you wanted to do it you had to look bored as if you weren't interested. If you showed you were scared, you'd had it. They'd tease you till you did it or went home.

One day Mark's dad took us fishing down at the canal. We went and it was quite good if you could beat the boredom. He gave us a rod each with a hook and a bit of cheese on the end but all you could do was sit there, holding the rod and looking at the float in the water. The water didn't even move and you weren't allowed to make a noise, or pretend to be Tarzan throwing stones at crocodiles or anything.

We couldn't help talking though and so his dad moved away up the canal for a bit of peace and quiet. I saw a better place to go and fish and ran up the bank. It was slippery and muddy after the rain, and I came across a bit of the path that sloped into the canal and I slipped and hit my head on the bank and was under.

It was weird. Through the dark green-brown water, long strands of weed waving up past me and bubbles coming out of my mouth. I didn't know what to think, I just watched. I wasn't even scared.

Then suddenly a hand reached under the water, grabbed me by the hair, pulled me right out of the canal and lay me on the bank, pushing me hard till the water came splashing out of my mouth and nose.

Then the policeman packed up all his fishing tackle in a bad mood and took me home. I was really glad that Dad wasn't there and they didn't meet each other.

God and Superman

I knew that God was massive and that he made everything and that if you truly believed in him and prayed to him loads and said how great he was then he'd give you anything because you had faith. I also knew that Superman was faster than a bullet and stronger than a special train called a 'locomotive' and best of all he could fly.

One day I had to go to the shops to get a loaf of bread, a pint of milk and some eggs. The shops were all in a row next to the newsagent's at the end of our estate. After I'd got the shopping I thought about the long walk home and had a better idea. Crossing the road at the pelican crossing, I went into the park opposite the shops.

Sitting on a bench for ages thinking about God and Superman I told God that I really, really believed in him with all my heart and had loads and loads of faith. Then I asked him to let me fly home like Superman.

I looked up and over the roofs of the shops to where I lived and guessed where my house was. I knew I'd find it just by looking down and seeing the big oak tree in our back garden.

I stood up on the park bench and had a quick look round to make sure nobody was looking at me because I knew that God didn't like it when loads of people saw his miracles. Clutching the bread and the eggs and the bottle of milk in the shopping bag with one arm, I stuck my other arm out straight just like Superman and jumped into the sky shouting, 'Up, up and away!'

I landed flat on my belly, broke the eggs and squashed the bread. The bottle of milk knocked the breath out of me.

I lay there still and quiet for a while, then I sat up and looked around to check and was glad that nobody had seen. Picking up the shopping, I walked slowly all the way home, fluffing up the bread as best I could and thinking of some story to tell about the eggs. God was rubbish compared to Superman. At least Superman never made promises he didn't keep – like everybody else.

My new mum

When Dad told us we were going to have a new mum I was a bit scared because we hadn't met her and I thought she might be like Carol – she might even be Carol.

'Where do you get new mums from, Dad?'

'Liverpool.'

She came to visit us one day and we all had to wash our faces. Luckily she wasn't Carol. She was Elsa and she was beautiful and really kind like Julie Andrews, and had a big laugh that made everyone else laugh as well. She was tall and had tall blonde hair and she smiled because she was happy, not just because she was talking to Dad's kids.

Dad had taken a job as a taxi driver in Liverpool and he had to go to this nightclub where our new mum was working as a dancer. Our new mum told the manager of that club it was dangerous for all the 'girls' to go home alone at night and if he didn't organise a taxi for them they were going on strike.

Dad was the taxi driver that picked them up and he took an

instant 'shine to her' and he made sure that our new mum was the last dancer to leave his taxi that first night.

They got married two weeks after they met and we all went to the wedding and so did our aunties and uncles and cousins and Nan and Grandad.

Dad wore a suit, Mum wore pink and I had a white shirt with a blue tie and short trousers that were ironed to give a sharp crease down the front and back. We stood on the steps of the registry office afterwards and had our photograph taken. It was brilliant and everyone was happy and excited.

She used to cook us meals that we ate at the table at the far end of the lounge that we now called 'the dining room'. We didn't eat in the pantry any more. She bought us new clothes, matching blue jeans, and long trousers, T-shirts and pyjamas. I loved my pyjamas because they were like a suit and they made me look like Simon Templar, The Saint from on the telly.

All that waiting around the window sill on my own before school was over when my new mum came. Dad didn't have to take Diane to her special school dead early, and she and Andy and me could be with our new mum and have loads of breakfast and big chats until it was time for us to go to school.

Our new mum was great, she'd been a photographer and had spent loads of time with the Beatles. She used to live in flats and then she'd just leave them with everything in them (even her pictures of the Beatles!) and just move on. I couldn't believe she'd left all her smart things in those old places and wished she'd kept them so I could see them and we could have them in our house.

She had been an air hostess as well and used to work for BOAC. She told us that all the air hostesses said it stood for

'Better Off On A Camel!' I thought that was really funny. Before that she was a dancer and she danced in Paris. I knew where Paris was because it was one of the capitals of the world. Capitals stood for big letters at the front of sentences, and also for big important cities that stood for countries like Paris, New York, Berlin and Liverpool.

Our new mum made Dad drive us all the way to Liverpool to see the Christmas lights. We all called Liverpool 'The Pool' like it was a mate of ours and it made me feel as though I was part of the big world. Another time she made Dad take us all to Liverpool airport and we stood up by the rail and watched airplanes taking off and landing. I was sad that we weren't going on an airplane but really happy when we had our lunch in the restaurant as a special treat with no washing-up afterwards.

Later that same day we all went on the ferry across the Mersey just like in the song and Diane leaned over to look at the water rush past the boat. The river looked just like washing-up water in the sink after a big dinner. Diane suddenly did one of her big laughs for no reason and her false teeth fell out and splashed into the water and she started crying till Mum comforted her. 'Don't worry, Diane, we'll get you new teeth.'

I was very happy with our new mum and I didn't think about our old mum very much any more.

Caught

In that long hot summer of 1969 Mum used to make us not watch telly all the time and she'd dress us in nothing but swimming trunks and send us out of the house to play with the hosepipe instead.

It was great fun getting your mates round and playing tag with the hosepipe because it was really cold when it first hit your warm, dry skin but then after a while you wanted to get caught with the spray just to cool down.

There were a couple of girls playing with us one day and I had an idea to go down to the shop and get some sweets. They said they had no money and I said that didn't matter. I'd been loads of times with Terry and he'd steal whatever he wanted. It was dead easy.

When we got to the newsagent's I took a Mars bar and, with nowhere else to hide it, stuffed it down the front of my swimming trunks then walked towards the door. Suddenly I felt the big hand of the newsagent on my shoulder.

'Come 'ere, you dirty little commie thief!'

I said I didn't know what he was talking about.

He pointed at the tell-tale bulge in the front of my trunks. 'What's that then, Scotch mist?'

He didn't want to touch the Mars bar but he said he wanted money for it and when I said I didn't have any he marched me all the way home to speak to my mum.

At home I was too scared to cry even, and the newsagent told my new mum what I'd done and she looked at the Mars bar now melting a bit in my hot hand and she spoke very calmly. 'I'm sorry, I must have forgotten to give him the money. Wait here and I'll get it for you.'

Maybe it was because Mum was so pretty or because she spoke so nicely with her Wallasey accent that the newsagent stopped being so angry and started mumbling about how hard it was to run a business with so many shoplifters around these days. Mum said it must be very difficult for him and told him that I was a good boy really and would never steal.

Eventually the newsagent turned to leave, patting me on the shoulder. 'It's all right, son, you're not banned from my shop. Just make sure you bring your money or your lovely mum along next time, eh?'

I hated him so I kept looking at my feet till he'd gone.

Mum got dead serious then, and told me that stealing was very bad and I could get into trouble and I should never do it again because it was wrong.

'Sorry, Mum.' I offered her the sloppy Mars bar, but she had to look away because she was smirking.

All my mates were waiting outside the house to see what would happen. I came out smiling. We got chocolate all over our hands and faces because the Mars bar was so soft, but that was all right because we could go and play with the hosepipe to clean ourselves in the sun again.

Mum told Dad about the Mars bar when he got home from work that night. He got dead angry and told me to go to my room.

I went upstairs to the room I shared with Andy and Diane, and waited.

I could hear them talking downstairs and then I heard Dad's big footsteps as he came up the stairs two at a time. He pushed the door open and closed it behind him.

'What's your game?'

'I'm sorry, Dad. It was an accident.'

Then he unbuckled his belt and drew it through the loops of his jeans and I got really scared. 'I didn't mean it. I won't do it again!'

Then he pushed the two ends of the belt together to make a mouth and pulled the two ends apart dead fast and the belt made five big snapping sounds as he spoke. 'Don't. Ever. Do. That. Again!'

From downstairs I heard Mum shout up with a sorry voice, 'That's enough, Dennis!'

I just stared at him because I didn't understand. He winked at me and spoke quietly. 'Behave yourself, all right?'

Then he left the room and closed the door. I sat on the edge of the bed and wished I had a belt so I could do that special trick.

The bald eagle

I was a bit scared of Dad's mate, Tommy the Bald Eagle. He was a scaffolder and his real name was Garfield. He had massive arms and a red face, and he wore a wig to hide his baldness and he talked in a deep, gravelly voice using only short sentences. He could talk with his teeth closed tight together. It was like he was always in a bad mood and it was a surprise whenever he laughed – which he did often in fact.

He and my dad were talking about work once and they

were swearing all the time – especially Tommy.

'You can't believe the fucking conditions, Dessie! There's fucking scabs and bleeding kids! Don't know their arse from their elbow! It's fucking dangerous, Dessie!'

I was listening to all this and I wanted to say something too so I spoke up: 'Bastards.'

Tommy stopped talking suddenly and turned on me looking horrified. 'What's that, Nicky? Did you hear that, Dessie? Bleeding swearing! I ought to wash his mouth out, don't you think, Dessie?'

'Aye, go on, Tommy.'

Tommy ran through and got a bar of carbolic soap from the kitchen sink and came back into the lounge and grabbed me and pushed the soap into my mouth.

It was horrible and I wriggled and pressed my lips closed, but it was too late, and it was over dead quick. Afterwards Tommy laughed and gave me a packet of biscuits, but the taste of soap stayed for ages.

Activists

Because my dad was a political activist he used to have to go out to pubs and have meetings. We used to get loads of visits from other activists and Mum didn't really like them. One that came round all the time was a big smiley man. Mum called him 'a wolf in a sheepskin coat'.

'He's just using you because you're a natural leader.'

'You don't understand, Elsa. Drop it, will you?'

Then she'd say her thing louder and he'd say his thing louder and I thought she must be stupid not to understand. I'd go outside and play under the carport till it was dark and there was something on telly we could all watch instead of shouting.

Sometimes us kids had to go with Dad to his meetings in a pub called the Bull and Stirrup in Chester. We had to wait in the car for ages in the underground car park. It was a big place like a concrete cave and there were echoes with voices or footsteps in them. Through the back windows of the pub we'd sometimes see the shadows of people moving about but we could never know what they were doing so we'd have to guess. Sometimes a door would open and a man with an apron would step outside and have a fag. Sometimes a car would come in and park or another would leave. But apart from that nothing much happened.

We had to keep the car doors closed, but we could have the window open if we needed air – which we did. Diane and Andy used to get really bored and there'd be fights. Dad always promised us he'd bring us pop and crisps when the meeting was over, and left us with a serious look and another promise: 'Behave yourselves. I won't be long.'

But he was. He was hours. By the end, when he came back, Diane and Andy would be asleep all over me in the back seat.

After the meetings, Dad would get back to the car and mostly he'd be in a good mood, which meant they must have had a good meeting. I think Dad liked being an activist. When he and Mum argued about it, she'd say he should take more interest in his own family and kids, and he'd say he was doing it for all the kids of the whole country. I felt a bit jealous. Why should he do stuff for all the kids of the whole country when he didn't even know them? Dad said that was easy: 'That's what working-class people do,' he said. 'They look after each other.'

Most of the time he forgot the crisps and pop, too.

Wizard

There was a comic called *Wizard*. Somebody would buy it and we'd all share it, or you could find them for next to nothing in junk shops. I liked the word 'wizard' and I liked what wizards were – wise and kind old men with big sticks. They could do magic, ride horses, cast spells and fight really well. Wizards always won in the end because they had 'good' on their side. Dad said that if you had 'good' on your side you couldn't lose. You might lose the battle but you wouldn't lose the war.

When it came to Hallowe'en there was a big fancy dress competition at school and everyone could enter and there'd be a prize for the best three. Mum got straight to work making me a wizard's costume on our dining table. She told me that to win the prize I had to walk and talk like a wizard, I had to 'be' a wizard. I practised a bit in the lounge and she told me how to be even better. I had to bend my back and make my face angry and put on a deep voice and make up spells. I felt all right about doing it in the lounge but I wasn't sure about doing it in the big hall at school in front of the whole world.

I asked my dad what he thought. He dropped the newspaper from his face and watched me for a moment before commenting, 'You look a right lemon.'

We had to go to the school in the night and the sky was black and blue and it smelled like it was going to snow or maybe even hail. Shuffling along next to my mum, I practised walking and talking like a wizard. When we got near the school all the lights were on and it looked sort of special and a bit scary and I didn't want to go in, but Mum just laughed and kissed me on the head.

The audience was full of parents and little kids too small to enter the competition. There were millions of us up on the stage where the headmaster did assembly. He said some things that made the parents laugh and then we all had to set off across the stage leaving little gaps between us.

It was my turn to walk across the stage as a wizard. My heart was going mad. I was bent nearly double and my face was all twisted and I mumbled and moaned and cast spells as I went, keeping my head down and watching my feet.

I was doing all right until a fairy in front of me did a little twirl and the audience laughed and clapped. Then a goblin stopped in the middle of the stage and opened his arms and said something to the audience and they all shouted happily and clapped. I was behind them thinking, 'What can I do?' I couldn't think of anything except a twirl or opening my arms and casting a spell at the audience, but that had already been done by the fairy and the goblin and people hated copycats, so I just stuck to my act, and kept my head down muttering, 'Look at me, look at me, I'm a wizard!'

My face was really hot the whole time and I was really glad when I got to the other side of the stage and I could go behind the curtain and it was over.

Then we had to wait at the side by the big curtains while the headmaster said how hard it was to decide and then he gave the prizes to three other kids, including the fairy and the goblin, and I felt like a right lemon.

Later we all went outside to the sports field and they lit this massive bonfire and set off fireworks and that was ace. Me and my mates ran around the bonfire outside the safety tape and had wizard fights and pretended the fireworks were our weapons.

I stopped running and looked through the flames of the bonfire, and felt the front of my face go all warm. Past the bonfire I could see Mum and Dad leaning into each other and holding hands. Mum's head was resting on Dad's shoulder, and I thought that was magic.

Drive-by

Sometimes when Dad's car was going slowly uphill we all had to push from the back. We'd have to lean on the front seats and shout, 'Puuuuuush!' It always worked; we always got to the top of the hill.

Because I got car sick, Mum used to tuck flowers into the little pockets on the back of the front seats to make it smell nicer. I used to travel feeling sick, and watching the flowers die. The worst was when we stopped at petrol stations and you'd have to smell the fumes.

Once we were all going on holiday down to Devon. We had to go in the car. We were on the motorway and I'd eaten too much and I needed to go.

'Dad, I've got to do a number two.'

'Can't you hold on?'

'Are we nearly there?'

'No.'

'I've got to do a number two!'

Dad pulled over onto the hard shoulder and told me to open the car door and squat down next to it. He promised me no one would see me because the car would shield me from the passing cars.

Pulling down my trousers and undies, I squatted down and started to go, then Dad drove off, leaving me in full view of all the traffic. He was laughing, and Mum was shouting, 'Dennis, Dennis, stop the car!'

He stopped not far away and I ran with my trousers down by my ankles till I got back inside without even wiping my bum.

I hated my dad for doing that but I loved my mum for making him stop.

Champion

I let my hair grow long when everybody was growing theirs. One day in school the teacher told me to stand up and he made fun of my hair in front of the whole class.

'Isn't it about time you had a haircut, laddy?'

I told Mum, and she told Dad.

The next day Dad's silhouette appeared through the frosted glass of the classroom, striding down the corridor. He opened the door and walked in without knocking or saying, 'Excuse me.' He stood inside the doorway and looked at the teacher. 'Can I have a word with you, mate?'

'Erm, well –'

'Let's step outside, shall we?'

The teacher looked nervous. He scanned the room and stared at his chalk like he didn't know what to do with it any more. Eventually he dropped it in his pocket and followed Dad out into the corridor.

They were out there for ages. It was like a shadow puppet play through the frosted glass and we all watched as Dad pointed his fingers at the teacher and the teacher backed off. Then Dad left and the teacher waited a moment before he came back into the classroom and looked around for the chalk that we all knew was still in his pocket.

It was brilliant. For the rest of the lesson I could do what I liked.

That night we all sat round the dinner table and Dad told us what he had said and how the teacher had stuttered and stammered all over the place. 'I told him if he ever took the mickey out of our Nicky's hair again I'd be right round.'

'Oh, Dennis!'

'What did he say, Dad?'

Dad put on a poncey, scared voice. 'No no, Mr Warren, there's nothing wrong with long hair, I often wear my hair quite long as well!'

We all roared with laughter, and I filled with pride.

Front door man

The tastiest milk was sterilised with the steel tops – 'sterry' we all called it. Only one of our mates' mums had it, and she lived on the other side of the estate, but it was worth the walk. We all loved beans on toast, too, and Carnation evaporated milk with jelly, and chip butties, which were nearly too much, but you never wanted them to end and you'd eat them so quick you could hardly breathe afterwards. A man used to come round in a van and sell Lucky Bags. The sweets in there were always worth saving till bedtime. Suck them slowly under the covers for sweet dreams.

But vegetables were horrible. White sloppy runner beans kept me staring at my plate for hours on end, and that's what I was doing one evening when there was a knock at the front door.

Dad bounced up from the table and made his way to the front door as if he was expecting it. Diane had already finished her dinner and she was busy breaking something up in our room. Andy was staring at his plate, too. Me and Mum sat at the table not moving and not making a sound so we could hear what was being said at the front door.

When Dad came back he said he had to go out for a bit.

Mum threw her serviette onto her plate and left the room and ran upstairs. 'Not again!' Dad looked at me and at my plate. 'Finish them beans before I get back.'

Then he took a deep breath and pulled his coat on and left the house.

Looking at the ghostly white beans on my plate, I smiled. I had a thousand ways to get rid of those beans and not one of them was going down my throat tonight.

Birthday

My first birthday with my new mum I was eight years old and I got loads of presents.

I woke early and discovered that I had a Dalek suit just like on *Dr Who*. Daleks didn't scare me all that much; most of the time when they tried to shoot people they missed. The scariest thing about them was that they-talked-like-this-with-tinny-robot-voices. These voices were so scary that we used them in the playground. My Dalek suit had a plastic dome helmet with a death-ray gun turret and a plastic sheet with studs painted on that went down to my feet. Thrilled, I quickly got dressed up and waddled out of the house before anyone else was even awake. I headed down the alley, hoping to find some earthling I could terrify, and practising, 'Ex-ter-min-ate, ex-ter-min-ate!'

I was an all-powerful, protected and fearless alien on a mission to take over Ellesmere Port. But it was short-lived. I couldn't see where I was going and got about ten yards up the alley before I tripped and crashed into the brick wall and cracked the helmet. The Dalek was dead.

Heading straight back home with the helmet in my hands, I climbed into my second present, a totally brilliant pedal-powered go-cart. I set off from the front door and headed for the road. I raced along, curling and whirling to avoid the dog turds, and made it to the far pavement before nose-diving off the high kerb into the road and cracking the axle, snapping the go-cart almost in half. I got out and dragged it back to the house.

They were the best birthday presents I'd ever had and it was all over before my friends had even started their breakfasts.

I sat on the scratchy sofa and Dad came down and put the kettle on as I was looking through my birthday cards on the mantelpiece.

'Let's see your pressies then.'

'They broke.'

'Jesus Christ.'

I went back to my cards and he pulled a couple of mugs from the cupboard to make tea, shaking his head.

That weekend Mum organised a birthday party for me. I got new clothes, and these weren't even counted as presents!

Dad was away at a meeting that Saturday but Mum told me not to worry and said I could have as much fun as I liked, but I wasn't allowed to throw the trifles at anyone. I hadn't thought of that and promised I wouldn't.

As soon as the party started, I picked up a couple of trifles, ran out into the back garden and threw them at my friends. Mum didn't say anything; it was my birthday.

Historic day

When Mum got married to Dad she already had a whole family of her own. She had two daughters, Norma and Elaine. She was a bit older than my dad and had had her children very young, so they were already grown up. Elaine even had two kids of her own.

Things weren't going very well with Elaine though. There were lots of stifled tears and muffled conversations I wasn't allowed to listen to between Mum and Dad about Elaine.

We visited Elaine and her husband once. Her two kids were called Katy and Christopher. Katy was about two and half and Christopher was in a cot and he was smaller than a doll.

The living room was very small and dark because the windows were dirty and the wallpaper and the carpet had these busy patterns so that you couldn't really see anything without seeing everything at the same time.

While the grown-ups got on with their talking, I played peek-a-boo with Katy. She'd crawl behind the sofa from one end to the other, then I'd do the same in front of the sofa and when she peeked her little curly head round I'd shout,

'Peek-a-boo!' and she'd collapse in a fit of giggles and disappear again.

Only Katy and I were having any fun. Everyone else was stiff and uncomfortable. You could always tell when Mum was uncomfortable because she smiled a lot with her mouth, but her eyes were cold.

The telly was on the whole time. Most often the telly was on when there was tension in the family so that everyone could look at the telly instead of looking at each other, but today the telly was on the whole time we were there because this was a really 'historic day'.

Katy and I had to stop playing. I understood this but Katy didn't. I had to watch her being ripped off the floor and put into her cot by her horrible dad and then we all had to watch the American astronauts landing on the moon. It took ages.

After the Americans landed, we stood up, said goodbye and left.

It turned out that Katy's dad used to tie her up in her cot and put sticking plaster over her mouth to keep her quiet when she cried and he was trying to watch telly.

For me, the day the Americans 'splash-landed' back onto Earth was much more exciting than the moon landing because we all watched it shouting and screaming and playing peek-a-boo in our own house with our new brother and sister, Christopher and Katy, who had come to live with us for ever.

My dad had rescued them, and I was going to make sure they didn't feel sad or lonely or not wanted ever again.

Shifting allegiances

There was this girl called Sharon and she had a little brother called Lester. Sharon was fat and dead funny and I liked her. We were mates.

Then one day I fell in with a new crowd and this other girl called Frances was the leader. I sat with them all one day for school dinners, and Frances showed me a trick. I had to stick my finger into her closed palm and she pulled her thumb saying that was the toilet flushing and then I had to smell my finger, and sure enough, it smelled like poo.

We were all laughing when Sharon came over looking for me. But before she got to our table Frances said I shouldn't mix with Sharon because she stank. It was a hard moment. I liked being in this gang, but didn't want to hurt Sharon. Staring at my plate of food, I could feel Sharon staring at me until eventually she went away.

Frances said Sharon and Lester came from a poor family, poorer than all the rest of us even. It was all right to be a lot of things but it was really bad to be the poorest because then you were 'common as dirt' and you had to leave those people behind or they'd drag you down and borrow things off you and never give them back.

Holly Bank

Mum thought it was bad that I couldn't read properly at eight years old. She used to send me to my bedroom with a library book. I'd stumble through it for an hour or so, quite enjoying the bits I could understand – the pictures – then I'd go down and tell Mum I'd read the chapter. It all fell to pieces when she gave me a test.

'What happened in the chapter?'

'Er …'

Back to the book.

My maths was bad, too. I couldn't read, I couldn't write and I couldn't do sums. Mum said she wanted to put me into Holly Bank, a private school in Chester and Dad said we couldn't afford it.

So Mum got a job as an Avon lady and said she'd pay for it.

'You're going to turn him into a right ponce!'

'Dennis!'

'He could get a perfectly good state education if he'd bleeding well concentrate!'

'He needs special attention. Just for a year.'

Then Dad threw up his arms and slapped his newspaper down and walked out of the room.

I wasn't happy about leaving Terry behind, but I did like my new school uniform, which even had a blazer and a cap. I looked quite posh, even though I wasn't really.

'He looks a right Herbert.'

'Leave him alone. You look very smart, Nicky.'

I also loved taking the big green bus to Chester every day, there and back. Mum took me herself a few times till I got used to the route, and then she gave me a brand-new leather satchel with my name and address written in big clear letters under the inside flap with a sixpence taped next to our telephone number in case of emergencies. I'd lift the flap of that satchel and smell the leather mixed with the smells of banana and Marmite sandwiches on the bus to Chester.

Holly Bank was like a mansion with loads of rooms leading off a big hallway and a double staircase leading upstairs. In my new class there were only about fifteen kids instead of more than thirty at my old school. The teacher read *The Water Babies* and we'd have to follow the words in our books, which took ages. I'd sit at the back getting tired in the hot sun coming in through tall windows, which looked out onto the garden where we did our PE.

We used to have packed lunches made by our mums. You'd be starving by the time it came to open your desks and get down to eating. I'd get a Blue Ribbon chocolate bar as well as the banana and the Marmite sandwiches, cut up into four squares. We'd all swap to try and get the best lunch.

I didn't really make any friends – I didn't talk much because my voice was different from everyone else's – but I sat next to one kid who had a spare seat at his desk and we became friends, at least I thought we did. But one day the teacher said we could all move to a new desk to sit next to whoever we wanted. Everybody moved except me. I thought the kid next to me liked me but it turned out that he didn't because he moved.

It was horrible, it was really hard to breathe and I could feel my eyes prickling, and I buried my face in my project book.

On Wednesdays I had to stay late after school and sit in a small classroom on my own with a teacher who gave me sums to do. I sat there with a numb brain, swallowing my spit and trying not to become more and more nervous as he got more and more impatient. There were also extra lessons in reading and writing and they went a bit better.

Later that year I found myself sitting behind a beautiful girl with long, silver-blonde hair. Settled in by now, I was even a bit relaxed, and was passing secret messages around the class, digging my name into the soft wood of my desk top with the point of my protractor and filling it in with my ink pen, and sneaking bits of lunch when the teacher wasn't looking.

I was happy at Holly Bank and in love with the blonde girl in front of me. She made my heart thump when she looked at me and I used to kick the back of her chair to get her attention then look away as if it wasn't me. She liked me too, I just knew it. Then one day, after I'd kicked her chair during story-time, she turned round quickly and calmly, looked straight into my face and said, 'You've got the ugliest eyes I've ever seen.'

The school smelled of wood and fruit and oils and ink and hot woollen blazers baked by the sun and moistened by the rain. It smelled like magic, it smelled like *The Water Babies*.

Missing the bus

I made friends with a girl and her younger brother who used to travel with me from Ellesmere Port. We weren't in the same class because the girl was older and her brother was younger than me.

I liked her a lot, I wasn't bothered all that much about her brother, but I liked her; she made me feel grown-up. I liked spending time with her and talking about our school in Chester as if it was completely normal.

One day, we were waiting for the bus outside school and she asked me if I wanted to go with them to the corner shop to steal some 'bonbons'. They were hard little toffees like acorns covered with a yellow or white icing sugar coating. I thought it would make me look more grown-up if I said no. 'I think stealing is wrong,' I said.

They were teaching us about right and wrong and God and evil at school and I liked the stories and I could see what they were getting at and so I thought it would sound good. It didn't work.

The younger brother tried to persuade me to go with them, but his older sister butted in angrily. 'If he doesn't want to come with us he doesn't have to.'

And off they went. I knew I'd lost a chance to be close to her in a real adventure and I felt stupid.

With only moments to go before the bus arrived I raced across the road and down the side street where they had gone. Then I realised that I didn't know where the corner shop was.

It was nowhere to be found among the redbrick houses of this terrace and so I took a left and another left and scampered down two stranger, quieter roads until I was back near where I started on the wrong side of the road watching my bus pull away from the stop.

I did what any reasonable kid would do in the circumstances – I panicked.

I ran across the road shouting after the bus, and then over the roundabout with the fountains in the middle and a car even skidded and honked but I didn't look or listen, just ran and ran and watched the bus getting further away.

I stopped at the third bus stop away from school, scared and out of breath. At the bus stop was an old man. He didn't look right – his face was all red and craggy and his clothes were a bit dirty – but he came up to me and started talking about helping me.

There was a phone box over the road and I told him I had to call my mum and dad.

'Easy does it, lad, I'll help you get over the road.'

I was about to go with him because I didn't know what else to do. Then this really lovely woman came up to us and put herself between me and the old man. 'Excuse me, can I help?'

She was dressed just like my mum, she was tall like my mum and she smelled nice, too. She thanked the old man and said she'd look after me. And she did. She asked me to go home with her and I didn't even think twice about going.

It was a short walk to their house and they had two daughters who went to Holly Bank as well. They were both a bit older than me and so beautiful it was almost painful to look at them. They were like angels in their after-school dresses and they were both really nice to me and they wanted to play with me.

We went out into their garden, which was even bigger than our whole playground at school, and we played on their Space Hopper. I loved them both, but I loved the older one most.

Later we had supper and their dad came home and he was wearing a suit. My dad had a suit but he didn't wear it much, only when he went out for a drink or to get married.

They were all really nice, their house was beautiful, their

food was delicious. I remembered all the things my mum had taught me about how to answer a question politely, how to eat properly, especially soup where you had to tip the bowl away from you. You had to wait until you'd swallowed your food, then you had to dab your mouth with your serviette before you answered a question because this was polite, and also it gave you time to think up a good answer.

If I made myself just the same as them then they might like me and I'd be able to come back and maybe even live with them like a brother. That thought made me a bit nervous but I couldn't help it.

They told me that they had phoned my mum and dad – they called them my 'parents' but I knew what they meant – and that they were coming to get me as soon as my dad had finished work.

My heart sank. I didn't want to leave, and most importantly I didn't want my dad to come to this house in his jeans with his long hair and rust all over him. I thought he might look around their house and say something wrong, like, 'Aye aye – I think we'll have to share a lot of this stuff with the factory workers, don't you?'

I was quiet for a while just hoping he'd change into his suit before he came. It was a strange feeling. I loved my dad, but felt worried about him. He wasn't normal. He didn't say or think normal things and he didn't care what other people thought. He wouldn't fit in. I felt like a dirty traitor thinking like this but I couldn't help it. I just wanted to be normal like these people.

You had to fit in, that was the most important thing. If you didn't fit in you'd stick out and people wouldn't like you and they'd make fun of you and be cruel and then send you away.

And if they didn't like my dad how was I going to marry the older sister?

When Mum and Dad came to collect me it was all fine. My dad was so handsome and relaxed that everyone liked him, and Mum talked just like the woman. They had a nice chat while Dad talked to the father in the suit without mentioning communism or killing the Queen or sharing out their lovely ornaments and making him work in a factory. I talked to the girls, saying goodbye for ages. We promised we'd see each other in school.

The next day, after assembly I did see the older sister, for the last time. I was standing on the black-and-white tiles in the hallway outside my classroom and she was climbing the big curly-whirly staircase up to hers. We looked at each other for a moment, then she disappeared. That was that.

I looked for her after that but never saw her again. Although I didn't know it we were about to move to another country altogether – Wales.

Glan Gerrionedd

The Getaway

In the autumn of 1988 I took my father to an old Welsh mountain hideaway called Glan Gerrionedd. It was a near-derelict two-storey farmhouse with electricity but no water supply and, as such, a challenge for a man with Parkinson's.

Nevertheless, fifteen years after his arrest and imprisonment, I wanted to spend some time alone with him. I had this idea that we could talk.

Dad was always good at talking. He could talk passionately and brilliantly about politics and he could make you bark with laughter at his anecdotes, but he faltered into a wary silence when it came to issues that were more personal or less entertaining. I wanted to dig around in the soft bits that I knew were in there somewhere.

The farmhouse was spectacularly set on the edge of a steep pine forest leading up to a deserted slate mine complete with a cave of cathedral proportions. The front of the house boasted a generous veranda looking over a windswept, slate-grey lake reflecting the nearby mountains.

The inside was like a 1940s time capsule with dark wood floors and wall panels as well as an assortment of ancient floral upholstered furniture shredded and worn over years of occasional but enthusiastic use. There was a patterned tile floor in the hall, with rough hooks on the walls for hanging coats, and the two front rooms upstairs and down each had fireplaces and looked out onto the lake through small wooden windows painted fast to their frames. The back room downstairs had a grimy slate floor leading out to a kitchen and a scullery and these rooms were echoed upstairs by a third bedroom and a spartan bathroom.

It had the kind of comfort that you only really relish after a day in the driving rain, but there was plenty of that type of weather to make almost every return a welcome experience.

My dad was nearly fifty-one years old by then, long divorced from my stepmother, Elsa, and courting a new girlfriend. But for the next week it was just him and me. In that Welsh retreat, with its stark, barren beauty and its unpredictable climate, I became his nurse, administering his many pills throughout the day and raising cheerful fires in the old grate in the evening.

I had finished college and had a pretty decent degree in English but didn't know what to do with it. Most of my friends had moved on and I was writing stories at night and working on a building site as a chain boy during the day – hammering pegs into the earth and holding poles for the engineers who stood on the smart side of theodolites and told me to keep still. It was the kind of work normally done by pubescent kids. The chief engineer on the site was a gentle Iraqi and he was forever perplexed as to why I was doing such work. I could never give him a straight answer because I didn't know, I just liked being on building sites.

With my dad over that week I wanted to assemble the few and varied snapshots of my childhood recollections into something that made sense. For that I needed his help. On the first night, fuelled with Scotch, I pressed him about my birth mother.

'What was she like?' I asked.

He sat huddled in his padded anorak with his feet swaddled in two pairs of socks, his toes flexing in front of the fire. He looked at me with his bright light-blue eyes and pondered for a moment before muttering, 'Fiery.'

This was all I got on that first evening.

The next day I decided to test the limits of his disability, which came and went with irregular monotony. I said it was his turn to fetch the water from the lake in the twenty-gallon drum. He laughed at this and it took a fair bit of cajoling before he was inspired to utter his majestic roar and hurl himself out of the armchair to amble down the hill to the lakeside in a moment of bravado.

Standing at the edge of the lake with the oily sump of a sky overhead reflected in the slate grey of the lake surface, I urged him on: 'Go-aarrnn!' He waded out past the shingle shore and the water lapped over his wellies as he stooped to fill the drum.

'Go on, you lazy bastard, right to the top.'

'You cheeky bleeder.'

When the drum was full he began to make his way back to shore. And then he froze.

I watched as his wide shoulders shrank into a hollowing chest. His knees began to buckle and a low groan sailed across the surface of the indifferent lake.

I tried to make light of it and encourage him to reach the shore, but in the end there was nothing for it but to go in and guide him back. Removing my boots and socks, I rolled up my jeans and waded in to get him. I was doing him a big favour, and in return determined that he would have to be a lot more forthcoming in response to the list of questions I had.

New home

We moved to Wales in 1970 when I was nine. On the day we left Malpas Road to 'get our own house' I went out into the back garden to look at the big oak tree for the last time.

I wandered round the edge of the garden. Round and past the brick wall of the alley and the concrete slab wall that divided our garden from the neighbour's. Looking down, I saw a tiny oak tree sprouting up from the ground. I was really happy then. The old oak tree wouldn't be alone because it had a little one to keep it company.

After a while Dad came to get me. 'Stop making a meal of it and get a move on!'

It took a long time to get to Prestatyn on the coast of North Wales, so Dad had to sing to keep us quiet. Somehow he got to know about the girl with the yellow dress in the next estate and he made me tell him her name. Then he started singing, 'Michelle, my belle ...' I didn't mind really and started to sing along as well. But then he stopped singing and started laughing. 'Let's face it, Elsa, he can't sing.'

I stopped singing. I didn't want to do things I couldn't do.

We had already taken a trip to see our new house before it was even built. It was going to be in a row with loads of other houses that weren't built either. Even the road wasn't finished, and it looked like the pictures about the war with all the houses split in half and rubble everywhere. Terry and I couldn't work out why I was leaving Malpas Road for a war zone, but we promised we'd visit each other loads, which of course we never did.

When we got there on the day that we had to move in it was all finished (except for the front and back garden, which were just mud) and we all ran up the stairs and bagsied our bedrooms. In the end I had to share with Andy, which I did for years. He was even more fed up about it than I was, especially later.

That first night in our new house was dead exciting because there were boxes everywhere and nobody could find anything. We couldn't even cook so we got biscuits and a special cheese called Cracker Barrel that tasted like smoke and we all ate as much as we wanted except Diane who wouldn't stop if you didn't tell her to.

Then Mum got out something she called a 'ouija board' to see if we were going to happy in the house. Dad said she was mad and it was all a load of rubbish but she made him stay.

We all had to be quiet and Mum put a glass on the middle of this board thing and we had to hold hands and then Mum spoke:'Is there anybody there?'

Suddenly all the lights went out and Dad sprang up like a cat and ran up the stairs four at a time, yelling all the way, 'Jesus Christ, Elsa!'

The next day we were off down to the beach to look at the sea. It was the colour of wet ash. Mum and Dad walked along the shore hand in hand, with Christy and Katy in their arms, and Diane tagged along with Andy.

I was the only one who was free because I was the biggest, the oldest. I ran ahead on the hard, wet sand, seeing how far I could go before Mum shouted and told me to come back. The trick then was to lag behind and pretend to be looking at worm coils in the sand. That way I could really be out there on my own.

Skipping round Mum and Dad, kicking up tufts of sand, I asked loads of questions about the sea, including, 'How cold do you think the sea is, Dad?'

'I'll show you.'

He took me by one arm and one leg and lobbed me into the surf. It was so cold it was unbelievable.

All the sea and the sand rushed up my nose and down into my clothes. It felt like I'd been in ages but it must have been only a few seconds. Mum went mad and told Dad he was cruel, but I said it was all right because I didn't want them to shout on our first day in our new house. At least I was the first of the family to get into the Atlantic Ocean.

We had to go home then because I had 'deep shivers'. That's what Mum called them.

Big head

Mum was very interested in our education so before we moved to our new house she had found out what the local schools were like. I wasn't going to Holly Bank any more because I could read now and it was too far away. On my first day in my new school I had to go in and see the headmaster in his office. He sat behind his big desk in front of the window, and I perched on a big chair with my toes nearly touching the floor.

It was bright outside so I couldn't see his face properly, just his big hair with light shining through it. He asked my name and where I came from. I thought he should have known that already, but told him anyway. Then he nodded wisely, as if he knew all about Ellesmere Port.

'Ah yes, where they make all the cars. British Leyland, isn't it, or is it petrochemicals?'

It was the first time I'd heard that they made cars in Ellesmere Port, and I'd never heard of petrochemicals but I pretended I knew. 'Yes.'

'Well, I just wanted to say welcome to our school and I hope you'll be very happy here.'

And then he let me go.

I'd never really thought I wouldn't be happy in this new school but after that I worried a lot because what if I wasn't happy? What if everybody hated me and I didn't make any new friends?

Men at work

From our gate you could turn right down the road to the big field, or left down to the road that led up to town or down to the promenade. One day Mum let me take Dad's sandwiches to him at work. He and his mates were building the sea wall to protect all the people from floods and tidal waves as well as a new amusement arcade where people could go and have fun.

I saw him before he saw me. He looked ace. He was studying big drawings on blue paper, 'the plans' they were called, and he was explaining what they meant to some of his mates because he was the only one that could read plans.

He smiled when he saw me and he said, 'All right, mate?' Then he turned to all his mates. 'This is my lad, Nicky.'

They all turned to look at me and said, 'All right, mate.' It was so brilliant I could hardly breathe and couldn't stop grinning, but I kept a grip on myself and gave Dad his sandwiches.

Dad put a safety helmet on my head just like the one he was wearing and he showed me some tools and even let me hold a big cold piece of metal they use to keep scaffolding together.

'Can I keep it, Dad?' I asked.

They all laughed and said I'd get done for thieving and they laughed even more.

Dad wore a steel holster that hung loose over his jeans in his belt like a cowboy. He said it was called a 'frog' and that's where he kept his nips for nipping bits of wire to make the steel skeleton before the concrete got poured.

I wanted to stay and help but Dad said I had to go because he had to work. I couldn't wait to grow up so I could work with him.

Dad got that job because he used a different name and it took a whole week before the bosses found out who he really was and gave him the sack.

Flying Pickets

Dad was helping to organise men from all over the country to be flying pickets for the building workers' strike in 1972. I thought being a flying picket was like in your dreams where you're walking down the pavement and then you do a big jump and just float off into the sky. I saw my dad at the front of all these men walking up to building sites, then jumping into the sky to shout down at the scabs and the bosses. But it wasn't like that really. They just used buses.

There were lots more meetings at places like the Bull and Stirrup, but we didn't go with Dad any more. I missed it. I wanted to be there waiting in that parking cave with my arm out of the car window, making my hand into a fist and pretending to be a Fantastic Flying Picket and saying, 'Hey you – put your tools down and follow me!' in a solid Superman sort of voice.

Instead I had to stay at home with the other kids and do my homework.

Doing unto others

I asked too many questions at Sunday School. After a while the vicar got irritated and started ignoring my hand in the air.

Out of the two of them I liked Jesus much more than his dad because his dad seemed to get angry a lot and make bad things happen. He was very strict and a bit cruel, too. When I heard about the walls of Jericho I thought of all the mums and dads and their kids getting killed just because they got on God's nerves. I wanted to know why they all had to die like that but the vicar just told me that I'd missed the point and should pay more attention.

Then one day Mum and Dad asked me to make them a cup of tea. They were sitting at the dining table looking through bills and deciding how they were going to pay them. Dad was out of work even though he was busy organising the strike every day. But this was the weekend and he was home.

Listening to the kettle warm up, I was staring out of the back door at the sunlight warming the concrete path by the carport thinking about something that Jesus said. He said, 'Do unto others as you would have them do unto you.' Well, right then and there I thought I would like someone to do a cup of tea *and* coffee unto me so that's what I did unto my parents. I made them a cup of tea with a spoonful of coffee in it.

I put the two cups on the table and stepped back to the doorway to see if they liked this fantastic new drink.

They both took a sip at about the same time and their faces went a bit funny for a minute and they looked at their cups and at each other and then at me. 'What's this, Nicky?'

I told him what Jesus had said and Dad put his cup down and looked at Mum. 'Jesus Christ! You see what this Sunday School is doing?'

But Mum just laughed and said it was delicious.

I tried a cup myself later, and it wasn't really delicious at all. I thought maybe only women liked tea and coffee together, or maybe just real Christians who liked God more than I did.

Panto

Charlie was a tough case from school and wore shiny trousers that went two colours depending on the light. He lived in a house down on the council estates.

There were lots of gangs in those estates and you had to keep your head down and not look people in the eye otherwise they'd come over and stand in your way and say, 'What are you looking at?' It didn't matter what you said; they always had some reason to give you a battering. When that happened you just had to curl up into a ball and get it over with.

I liked hanging around with Charlie though because everyone knew him and his older brother, and nobody messed with either of them. Charlie talked a lot and knew how to get through fences and into sheds and other secret places. He was tough like I wanted to be.

I didn't really like visiting people at home when their parents were going to be there because you never knew what to expect. Charlie's parents shouted a lot, even when they weren't angry, and they didn't stand up when you came into the room, just stayed in their armchairs in front of the telly and gave you a nod.

They smoked all the time with ashtrays that had straps to keep them in place on the arm of the chairs. The place was a tip. They always had clothes drying in front of the fire and plates with toast crumbs and old cups of tea and the silver wrappers from meat pies with fag ends in them. Charlie's older brother just sat in front of the fire in his socks and he was about twelve and he smoked as well. I stayed near the doorway if I could but if they called you in to sit down you had to clear loads of newspapers and biscuit crumbs and dogs out of the way to find a space on the sofa.

Charlie's mum and dad talked loud and fast, and they were funny with their faces scrunched up the whole time because of the smoke from the cigarettes in their mouths going up into their eyes, making them squint and flap their hands a lot. My mum and dad didn't smoke at all.

One night we were going to the panto together and I had to go to Charlie's house first. I didn't want to be there and I wanted them all to hurry up, but it took ages before they found their coats and their shoes and then we all left. Charlie's older brother wanted to stay at home and keep his feet warm by the fire.

We were going in Charlie's dad's old car. He had to stick a big handle thing into the front of the car to wind the engine up. That took ages as well because he had to smoke at the same time and the smoke got in his eyes so he couldn't see what he was doing.

The panto was in a huge hall. There were millions of seats and it was already magic because of the air, which was full of people's breath perfumed by sweets and fizzy drinks. There were thousands of kids and hundreds of grown-ups. The kids were fidgeting and turning round and lobbing sweet wrappers at each other. It was just like church only not so boring. Me and Charlie swapped our sweets and chocolates, and I made sure that my mouth was full all the time so I didn't have to talk.

The show started. Great big blokes with hairy faces in fancy dresses with big boobs and loads of make-up were falling about the place and shouting, slapping, hiding and seeking, and telling big jokes and falling over again, and all we had to say was 'Behind you!' and 'Oh no, you're not!'

It was over too soon and we had all been laughing so much our faces were tired. Everyone in the whole place was happy and smiling. We drove home and even in the car we were all doing bits from the pantomime and by now I quite liked the cigarette smoke and only asked for a window to be opened because of my car sickness.

When I got home I did bits of the pantomime for Mum and Dad and it was ace to see them laughing.

Bali High

One day Dad didn't go picketing and instead he took me to see a movie. It was set on a tropical island and the white man who was the captain of the ship that was wrecked there fell in love with a beautiful dark woman. She was so beautiful that when you looked at her your face went hot.

She had dark hair with flowers in it and she smiled a lot and was very kind and spoke quietly while all around her other women sang 'Bali High' over and over and again like a chant till the man was desperate to get her on her own away from all the singing.

I thought Bali High must be the name of a really great school but Dad said it was the name of a country where the economy ran on child labour.

One day much later we all had to do creative writing in school. The idea was that we'd go off into groups and make a play. We knew what plays were; they were like what happened on telly only in real life. Charlie and I got together with three girls and we had to go next door to the empty classroom and make a play.

Charlie said this was brilliant because it was a way to 'get off' with the girls. I didn't really know much about girls except that they could be really cruel and say things and look at you in certain ways that made you feel horrible and sore and much worse than a real fight with a boy. But Charlie said you could stop all that just by kissing them.

I had learned to read by now, and I knew the whole of *Treasure Island* off by heart. I told Charlie all about it. Charlie said it sounded like a good story but there weren't any girls in it and plays had to have girls in them to be really brilliant.

So what happened in our play was that we were all shipwrecked on this desert island and we were all really tired and all we wanted to do was lie down and have a sleep. But the horror of the island was that there were no beds!

Charlie and I were really into this story and you could see that two of the girls were only pretending that they weren't into it as well. But the third girl wanted to do a play of her own. Fine, she was a spare girl anyway, so we let her go off into the other corner of the empty classroom to get on with making her own play.

Charlie and I decided that the best thing to do was to split up and look for beds. The first one to find any beds was to shout to the others. Brilliant. Off we went.

Finding a cardboard box, I unrolled it so it looked a bit like a bed and said to my girl that we should test it to see if it worked before we called the others. We lay down on it and it seemed to be working because before long we were holding each other quite tight and breathing each other's breath with her hair in my face and then we started kissing just like on TV except with our lips closed.

We kissed and kissed for ages till my lips got numb and I got bored and wanted to explore the rest of the island but she wouldn't let me because she said it was too dangerous and she started kissing me again.

Later we all had to show our plays to the rest of the class. Charlie and I became a bit nervous when we realised what we'd done and so we said our group wasn't ready but the spare girl said that she was.

She sat in a chair on the stage and stared at a cardboard box that she'd placed in front of her. We could all see the box, it had 'English Apple' written on it and the girl pretended that she was at home watching TV and she said, 'Oh look, Mum, it's *The English Apple*, my favourite programme.' There was something so brilliant about it that the whole class packed up laughing. She was brilliant. She was so clever that you almost couldn't believe she'd made it all up on her own.

By the end of her play I felt really bad about the way we'd

pushed her out of our group, and wanted to make her my girlfriend. I wanted to stay with her for ages and see what else she'd say that would be brilliant.

But she didn't even look at me. She was Julie and she needed nobody.

I thought about her all the time after that and used to look for her in the playground and watch her working in class. Once, when she was off sick, the whole class had to go round to her house, sit on the lawn of her front garden and look up at her in her bedroom window and sing a song to make her feel better. I concentrated really hard to make her look at me. It didn't work, but at least I knew where she lived.

It was easy to get to her house because it was on my way home from school and there was no wall or fence so you could just walk off the pavement onto her lawn and look up at her bedroom window.

Then, one morning, when we were all having our morning milk, the teacher stood by the big coal-fire stove and told us that Julia wouldn't be coming back to school because her parents were moving to Borneo and they were taking her with them.

I was gutted. Then we had to look at a map of the world until we all knew where Borneo was. I spent the whole of the day thinking about my English Apple and how I was going to lose her. Dad could see there was something on my mind when I got home and he asked me about it.

'What's the matter, mate, you look a bit fed up.'

'There's a girl leaving school and going to another country.'

'Oh aye, yeah?'

'I don't want her to go.'

'Do you know where she lives?'

'Yeah.'

'Well then.'

'What do you mean?'

'Use your loaf.'

The next afternoon on my way home I walked straight onto her lawn and stood there and looked up at her bedroom window. I didn't care what was going to happen. Behind me the traffic growled past and women walked by with prams or shopping and I just stood there.

Nothing happened. She didn't come to the window and smile down at me and throw down a rope so I could climb up into her bedroom where we could fall into each other's arms and plan how she was going to smuggle me into a cardboard box and take me to Borneo with her where I'd get a job on a boat and we'd watch each other grow up then get married.

That didn't happen. What happened was I never saw her ever again.

The last wave

It was very important to know loads of German war jokes. They weren't very good jokes but that didn't matter. I used to tell the same joke to Andy over and over, and he laughed every time as if he'd never heard it before. He never got bored of it. We'd be walking down to the shops or something and he'd suddenly say, 'Do the joke, do the joke,' and I'd do it and he'd open his mouth big and wide, and laugh with all the sunlight caught in his light-blue eyes.

When we used to go and visit Nan and Grandad in Chester at the weekend we used to drive past a little airfield where there was an old Spitfire near the fence. Spitfires were the greatest thing about the war because they protected the skies of Britain from the Germans who were trying to bomb all our chip shops.

There were loads of German planes and only a few Spitfires but our pilots were ace and theirs were crap and that's why we won. It was all about British Engineering, Grandad said. Grandad was in the war but he didn't talk about it much and I couldn't understand why but Dad said he knew: 'It's because he spent his whole time on the Falkland Islands in the Military Police arresting sheep!'

The other thing to look out for on that trip from North Wales to Chester was the old man who used to stand at the gate of the big house on the outskirts of town in a suit and tie and he'd wave as you went by. He was always there. We'd get close to the big house and look out for him and there he was and we'd all wave and his face would light up and he'd wave even harder.

Visiting Nan and Grandad was great because you could have loads of biscuits and you could go through their drawers finding secret things and ask if you could have them. You could take the newspaper into their bedroom and make airplanes and throw them out of the window and watch them fly. They lived really high up in a flat so the airplanes would go for ages. You could have races to see who was fastest going up and down the stairs. You could even go in the lift and press all the buttons and go screaming down other people's corridors and then escape in the lift before they came out.

When the visit was over we'd look out for the old man on

the way back as well and he'd still be there and we'd all wave again. It was like he knew when we'd be passing.

Then one day he wasn't there. It didn't make sense. When we left Nan and Grandad after our visit he still wasn't there. The gate was empty. I asked Mum and Dad what could have happened. Maybe they took him away for waving. Maybe you're not allowed to. Maybe there's a new rule or something. Maybe he's sick. Maybe we should go back and check up on him. But at the back of my mind I knew he was dead.

The big house he lived in was especially for old people and I knew that old people died all the time, they couldn't help it.

Maybe it was because I was a bit sad that this time when we got to the place where the Spitfire was parked Dad pulled in and spoke to one of the men and I was allowed to climb inside the Spitfire.

It smelled just like an old car. It was high up even when it was on the ground. There were loads of dials and switches that you were allowed to flick and tap and you could make noises like take-off and firing, and if you just looked up into the sky it was like you were defending Britain.

I thought about what it'd be like to be shot, the bullets ripping through the metal, tearing into your body and making you slump against the steering wheel, warm blood pouring out all over the seat. It wouldn't hurt. It'd be like being punched. You wouldn't even cry. You'd just remember the hateful eyes of the German pilot as he shot you and you'd go to sleep for ever. You'd try to eject and use the parachute, but you'd probably fall asleep before you finished, or you'd be just too sad to bother. You'd be asleep long before the plane hit the ground. Then everybody would be sad. Loads of people would come to your funeral and they'd shoot guns into the air and make speeches about how brave you were.

That's if you died in a Spitfire. But nothing happens if you die waving at strangers from the gateway of a big house on the outskirts of Chester.

Captain Archer

On the first day of the new school term we had a new teacher. I was sitting in my normal place at the back of the class near the aisle when he came in. I sat at the back because you could have more fun, it was nearest to the exit, and I had these stupid glasses for my bad eyesight so I could see the blackboard properly.

There was nobody to introduce him, he just strolled in. On his way past he turned round and looked at me straight in the face. 'What's your name?'

'Nick Warren, sir.'

'You look like an intelligent boy – I hope you don't disappoint me.'

I sat up straight and spent the whole rest of the day really concentrating on everything he said. I didn't want to disappoint him. He was called Captain Archer and he was a retired RAF pilot and he'd been in the war. It was like having someone walk out of the films right into your classroom.

He didn't teach ordinary lessons. When he was teaching geography he showed us photographs that he'd taken of the places he'd been to. If it was history he'd make it sound as though he'd been there and was telling a story. When it came to maths he gave us riddles to solve.

At the end of that first term I started sitting near the front of the class.

The next term we got an ordinary teacher and I moved back to the rear of the class near the exit but it was too late, I couldn't help being interested in lessons from then on.

Before Captain Archer left he'd given me his address and said I could visit him if I wanted. One Saturday I made Charlie come with me. Charlie wasn't keen because he didn't like teachers and he specially didn't want to see one on the weekend.

Captain Archer lived up near the mountain in a new housing estate of bungalows that were mostly for old people. We rode around looking for his house doing wheelies on the dead-clean jet-black tarmac roads and then we found it.

We parked our bikes and walked down the path. Charlie still wasn't keen and even I was a bit nervous now. Then we got near his front window and looked in. There he was, sitting on his sofa drinking a beer and watching a colour television with horseracing on it.

We'd never seen a colour telly except in shop windows! Charlie was dead keen to go in once he spotted that.

Captain Archer was surprised to see us but made us sit down and he gave us pop to drink and some biscuits to eat. We all sat there for ages talking about nothing; all we really wanted to do was watch the colour television. My dad used to watch the racing on Saturdays and I thought it was dead boring, but in colour it was great.

We stayed until the last race was run and it was time for the football results. I enjoyed listening to the football because they'd always mention Liverpool and eventually they'd mention Chester too, but you'd also hear these interesting places like Charlton Athletic, Wolverhampton Wanderers and Raith Rovers, and you'd wonder what it was like to live there.

In all the time we were there we never saw his wife. She didn't phone, he didn't talk about her, he didn't stand up and look through the window to see if she was coming home with the week's shopping. She didn't exist.

On the way home Charlie told me that his wife was already dead. I felt a bit sad about that for a while but at least he did have a colour telly.

When I got home I was dead excited and I wanted to tell Mum all about Captain Archer and his colour telly but she wasn't interested. She was too busy filling tea chests because we were moving again.

The colour of mountains

We had to sell our new house because we couldn't afford it any more and move into an old house in Meliden Road up near the mountain. It was in a bit of a state and needed loads of work, but Dad said we could fix it up in no time. The great thing was it had a basement with a door and if you bent over you could just walk into the house from the back garden. From the front windows you could see the big mountain that was at the back of Prestatyn. In paintings at school mountains were always brown or green but if you looked closely you could see all sorts of colours. Our mountain had loads of different shades of blue and purple as well as green and brown, and it looked ace when it got dark and the orange street lights came on.

From the front bedroom windows you could sit with your chin on the window sill and watch car headlights winding over the mountain roads. They were small roads up there where the houses thinned to almost nothing. That was wild land and you wondered who was driving up there and why.

When we moved in you could see your breath in front of your face at night and we all had to wear woolly gloves. It got dark early and from the back kitchen you could watch as the old railway track at the end of the garden vanished and the country blackness crept up like a blanket till there was nothing beyond your own small reflection in the big kitchen window.

Everyone was dead happy when we moved in except Mum.

'It's going to take a lot of work, Dennis.'

'Let's just move in first, shall we?'

Dad had been away being an activist for ages. He had to go out in the early mornings and get on a bus with loads of other strikers and travel round all the sites telling the lads they were being conned. Mostly they were scabs and lumpers and Dad said that meant they were mean little men working against their class.

Dad was good on the sites because he had a big mouth and he knew loads of things to say so they made him a leader and he had to stand on tables and up on scaffolding so they could hear him better. Dad was a good activist because when he finished talking most of the lads put their tools down and walked off the sites. I wondered who picked their tools up afterwards but Dad told me to behave myself so I didn't push it.

Dad was home for the whole of that first weekend. Home. That's what it was like. It had big old windows that didn't work properly but you could lift them up from the bottom and crawl outside if you put a stick there to keep it from falling. We didn't have curtains because all our old curtains were too small so the sun came in everywhere. The ceilings were dead high and you couldn't even touch them with a broom.

There was a dining room with a real fireplace like Aunty Gill's and a serving hatch through to the kitchen where you could pass plates and in the front there was something that Mum called a 'sitting room'.

It was a special room and we weren't really allowed in there. It was where the grown-ups were supposed to go and sit down and drink sherry out of crystal decanters and smoke cigarettes. At least that was what Mum wanted to happen. We didn't have decanters or cigarettes but Mum said we were going to get some soon. When I asked what you do in a sitting room she said that they would 'entertain' in there. I thought that meant they'd tell jokes or do bits from pantomimes but Mum said, no, it meant they would have adult conversations with friends and neighbours. It sounded dead boring to me but it never happened anyway.

Later Mum went out and bought textured wallpaper for it that Dad had to hang and I had to help him mix the glue. Then she had thick, thick curtains made and Dad had to hang them as well and you felt important just walking in there when no one was looking.

Dad brought home chestnuts in a big bag that winter and Mum taught us how to roast them on the fire. I was in charge because I was the oldest. You had to put them on an oven tray and wait for the fire to burn down a bit so it was just red embers and then put the tray on the embers and turn the nuts all the time so they didn't get burned. They made the whole room smell like a kid's story, like Christmas in films, like heaven. They tasted all right as well.

When we first moved into that house I smiled so much my face ached. My heart was full all the time. Everything was going to be great.

Andy's mate

I didn't know anybody who lived near our new house but Andy had a mate next door and he was weird. He'd mope around and speak slowly and quietly and say things under his breath, like, 'Let's go into the garden and dig graves.'

I didn't like him.

One day I was bored because Mum said I had to play in and around the house and I wasn't allowed out. She said this was because she might need me to help her with things, but really she was just lonely because Dad was picketing again.

So in my boredom I made a plan. From the back kitchen window I could see right down the garden to the old apple tree. From Dad's toolbox in the basement I got a very long piece of string. I tied one end to a brick, threw the string over a branch of the apple tree and pulled the brick up into the tree.

Then I stood at the far side of the tree and let the string go so that the brick fell. I did this a few times till I was sure where it would land. Then I took the other end of the string all the way to the kitchen and threw it through the window, tying it to the handle of a kitchen drawer and pulling the brick up into the tree.

I got a plastic cowboy and buried him up to his neck in the ground under the apple tree and told Andy to go and get his friend from next door and tell him that he'd found a dead cowboy buried under the apple tree. I told Andy to stay out of the way while his friend was inspecting the cowboy but I didn't tell him why.

The kid from next door came waddling over and went straight to the tree and fell to his knees to get a closer look at the cowboy. Looking on from the kitchen, I judged the moment and let the string go.

It was bad.

The brick dropped very fast and it hit the boy on the back of the head. He screamed and screamed. My nerves went and I ran down the garden and asked what had happened and had to hug the boy to help him stop crying then give him a cowboy to stop him from telling his mum.

I showed him where I kept all my cowboys and over the next few weeks he'd come round all the time and say his head was hurting and could he have another cowboy. Then he'd take my cowboys down to the old apple tree, bury them in the ground and pull the string to let the brick go. He squashed them over and over again until they were flat and useless.

I had to watch all this from the house. Andy and he would do the sound of the cowboys screaming as the brick fell and then they'd laugh like lunatics. In the end I had no more cowboys left, just a mangled collection of plastic.

The Banana Splits

In our old house Andy and me used to watch a programme on the telly every Saturday morning called *The Banana Splits*. Four daft creatures would shout and wave and then go and have loads of fun in a fairground. That was just the beginning of the show though. We'd only watch because we knew what was coming next – *Catch Candy*.

Catch Candy was all about this lad who ran away from home and had adventures. He nearly got caught every time but then he'd escape again at the last minute. What he didn't know was that there'd been a terrible mistake at home, and that his parents loved him and wanted him back.

We couldn't get that programme in our new house and Andy couldn't understand it. 'Where's *Catch Candy*?' he would ask.

'It's finished.'

'But it was on in our other house!'

'I know but it's finished now. It's not on any more. This other programme's on now instead.'

'I want to watch *Catch Candy*!'

In the end I'd have to give him a Chinese burn on his arm

to make him shut up about *Catch Candy*.

Then he ran away from home.

I came home from school and Andy wasn't anywhere. Mum was in the sitting room looking through magazines.

'Mum? Where's Andy?'

'He's run away.'

'You what?'

'Don't worry. He's only next door. He took a suitcase full of dirty laundry. I'm hoping they'll wash it all before they send him back.'

You could see into next door if you stood on the steps outside the kitchen and I watched for a while but I couldn't see him. He came home that night and when Mum opened the suitcase she loaded all the laundry into the bath to start washing it.

Then Diane ran away about a week later. That was more serious because Diane didn't go next door. Nobody knew where she went. We all had to go out and look for her. I found her hiding in a hedge near the railway line. She was just sitting there humming and it took ages before I could get her to come out. In the end I said dinner was ready and then she came.

I never ran away. I'd been away and I knew what it was like.

The monkey's head

Mum told me she was a feminist so it was important to her that I learned how to wash the dishes. I hated washing up because it took ages, it made your hands go all wrinkly and the kitchen was at the back of the house looking out over the dark garden out to the haunted railway track at the end, and the fields full of scarecrows and dead cowboy ghosts. It was best not to think about it.

The kitchen window was high off the ground because of the basement. I was doing the dishes there one night, listening to everyone watching telly, and was washing up as quickly as I could, trying not to look out of the window into the darkness.

Then suddenly a monkey's face smashed up against window – thud, thud, thud! I screamed and froze, then heard laughing. It was my dad. He'd sneaked outside by the front door, gone round the back and put a rubber monkey's head on a long piece of bamboo.

He moved back into the light spilling from the kitchen window then and dropped the bamboo stick. There were tears falling down his face.

I laughed afterwards and was glad that Dad had found something to cheer him up, but I didn't sleep much that night.

Hostage

Mum was sick of it. She said Dad didn't care about his own family. She said she was trying to make a home for his children and he wouldn't help her. He said they couldn't afford carpets and she said, 'Children need a proper home with carpets.'

I came home from school one day to find men putting carpets everywhere.

There was a carpet as soon as you came through the front door and it went all the way down the hall, up the stairs to the landing and along the hallway right to the kitchen at the back of the house. The sitting room had a carpet, the lounge had a carpet, even the dining room had a carpet. Upstairs all three bedrooms had carpets. There was even a carpet in the toilet and the bathroom. The whole house smelled of new carpets!

You couldn't help yourself, you had to just drop your satchel and roll around on the soft, sweet-smelling carpets. You'd have to take your shoes and socks off and feel the fluffy new carpet tickling your feet. For weeks none of us kids wanted to sit on the chairs or the sofa; we'd just sit or lie on the carpet.

Then the carpet man started coming round to ask for his money.

He never got angry. He and Mum would go into the sitting room and Mum would close the door. I'd make them tea and they'd talk about paying for the carpets.

One night he came round when Dad was home and I had to make three cups of tea. I kept quiet outside the sitting-room door so I could hear what they were saying.

The carpet man wasn't just a carpet man, it turned out; he was also a curate and he ran the church choir.

'Do you ever sing, Mr Warren?'

'Only on pay day. So I haven't sung for a long time.'

Looking through the crack in the door I could see Mum couldn't help smirking but the carpet man looked embarrassed and took a fresh interest in his cup of tea.

Andy started coming down the hallway to see what I was doing. I rushed away from the doorway so he couldn't give me away, and found him a bag of sugar and a teaspoon and left him to it.

Suddenly Dad called me. I went into the sitting room. 'This is Nicky, my eldest,' Dad said. 'He's got a lovely voice. You'd like to be in the choir, wouldn't you, mate?'

'What?'

He just looked at me with that little closed-mouth smile and winked at me, but I didn't wink back or even smile. I just stared. I hadn't sung since he told me to shut up because I couldn't sing 'Michelle my belle'. He knew I hated singing and now he was putting me in the church choir and the carpet man was going to teach me.

'So there you go – Nicky will sing in your choir as a sign of good faith until you get the rest of the money for the carpets.'

The man couldn't say anything but he looked at me as if he thought I wasn't worth a welcome mat let alone a two-storey house full of wall-to-wall shag-pile carpeting.

I looked at Mum but she was busy stirring her tea even though the cup was nearly empty.

I hated the choir. All the other lads were posh kids who I didn't know and they could all sing. They all spoke loudly with their eyes wide open and they used their hands and their lips a lot.

The carpet man used to get us in after school and on Saturdays for practice. He'd line us all up and step up to each of us and put his ear really close to your mouth to hear you singing and he always looked a bit sad when he put his ear by my mouth.

It wasn't all bad though. Weddings were great because you could watch the bride and groom looking more nervous than you were and women weeping in the front pews. You got paid for singing at weddings as well – 50p and a box of Quality Street.

But best of all was being on bell-ringing duty. The carpet man put me on bell-ringing most of the time because it wasn't so hard on his ears. You'd go up into the bell tower with another lad who couldn't sing and you'd have to pull the different ropes in turn.

The ropes had red plastic on them so you didn't hurt your hands. You knew that everyone could hear the bells all over town. They could hear them at the Territorial Army down the road and the hairdresser's up the hill and even at our house.

I used to walk home dead slow after weddings so I could eat all the soft Quality Streets myself and not have to share them. I knew that was wrong and not very Christian. I felt bad but I couldn't help it.

Big school

When I was eleven we all had to leave our little school because we were too big and we all had to go and be the smallest kids in the big school. We all knew that this meant we weren't allowed to wear our own clothes any more and that we'd have to wear school uniforms. We all moaned about this for ages but secretly I didn't mind. I liked it that we all had to wear the same because then you weren't looking at other people's trousers and wishing they were yours.

In the big school we got sorted into different Houses. Mine was called Neptune and Charlie went to Mars. I met a whole new bunch of lads as soon as we got sorted and some of them liked me straight away because I said we were lucky there wasn't a House called Uranus. We had timetables that we had to colour in for the different lessons and a map to show us where the classrooms were.

At break-time we hung around on the playing field, trying to get to know each other and to see who was going to be our leader. It wasn't going to be me because I wasn't big enough but I said more funny things and they all liked me. We undid the top buttons of our shirts and pulled our ties down and made the knots dead small and we were great.

Later in the term we were standing outside class, lined up against the wall waiting to go into History, and one of the lads started talking about Northern Ireland. He said the Irish had to be stupid to go around throwing bombs at each other. I kept quiet. Dad said they were in a war of liberation and there was nothing stupid about the Irish.

Special offer

The carpets were great, but with me as a hostage in the bell tower, Dad had to start forking out regular payments. Dad was on the dole and he was blacklisted as a troublemaker on every site he tried to get a start on. That was one of the reasons he was leading the strike so that union members could get work.

Food became a bit of an issue.

At night Dad would come home and Mum would cook him a 'proper dinner' but we'd all have sandwiches.

One day Andy got stroppy about his sandwiches and came right out with it: 'Why can't we have proper dinners as well?'

Mum told him. 'You get a cooked meal at school, that's why. Now eat your crusts.'

Then Dad did something really clever. It was a Saturday and we'd just come back with cramped stomachs from all the damsons we'd scrumped from the tree down the road, and outside our house there was this enormous van with four blokes carrying a chest freezer into the house.

They put it on the carpet in the dining room, a great white coffin, and then they filled it with meat and frozen vegetables and even ice creams and ice lollies. That night we all had our plates filled to the top and Dad didn't even try to steal my bits of meat like he usually did. We were all laughing with food in our mouths. The table was set properly again with a tablecloth and serviettes and there were even candles in the middle and we had ice cream for pudding.

We ate like that for a month. Every time we went to the freezer to get a meal or a treat we'd think how brilliant our dad was. His plan was genius. What he'd done was take a limited special offer from the freezer company: buy the freezer and get it filled with food for free. Dad had bought it on hire purchase – the 'never-never' – and he didn't pay a penny. By the time they came to repossess the freezer we'd emptied it.

Later Dad made Mum try the same trick in her own name but they'd changed the rules by then. You could only get the freezer full of food if you paid cash up front.

Tongue-lashing

One day Dad was home when we got back from school and he was in a really good mood. He said the strike was nearly over and it looked as though they were going to win.

'Does that mean you'll be home more?'

'It means I might get a job!'

'That's good.'

'Good? Is that all you can say!'

Then he shot off the chair and chased me through the house. He got me in the dining room and started tickling me like mad. I could hardly breathe I was laughing so much. I begged him to stop but then he pinned me down and licked me. He hadn't done this for ages and I'd forgotten how fantastically horrible it was. He stuck his tongue out and he ran it all over my face and my eyes and I could feel his bristles and smell his spit and I screamed and screamed but it didn't come out right because I was laughing so much.

Then the other kids came in and jumped on his back and he let me go and then it was their turn to get licked.

The wrecker

One day some men came from a national newspaper and wanted to interview my dad about the strike and the flying pickets. Dad was out picketing till late that night and they said they didn't mind waiting. Mum made them tea and sandwiches and they looked round our house. 'Christ, you haven't got anything!' they said.

I thought we had lots of things and didn't know what they meant. They were nice to us kids and they played with us and gave us sweets and things till Dad came home and they said they had to get to work.

When the paper came out Dad's face was on the front page under the headline 'THE WRECKER!' It talked about the Shrewsbury Pickets, how Dad was their leader and how they were nothing but gangsters. 'The right-wing Tory press,' Dad called it.

It was brilliant at first. My dad was in all the papers and even mentioned on the news on telly. All the kids at school talked about it, but after a few days they stopped talking about it, stopped meeting me at the gates and in the playground, and sort of stayed away from me in class.

Mum was worried, you could just tell. She kept us all out of school for a while. The phone was ringing all the time. At all hours of the day and night. Sometimes Mum would pick it up. She'd listen for a while and try to say something, then just gasp. Sometimes after she put the phone down she'd cry. It was the 'cowardly fascist bastards' calling.

I really wanted to know what they were saying. To know why they made my mum cry like that. I tried to get to the phone before Mum a few times but she screamed at me when I did. It made me want to even more, and then one day it rang when she was out shopping. She had told me not to answer the phone if it rang. I looked at it for a minute and then picked it up.

'We know where you live, you bastard. We're coming round there and we're going to kill your kids and rape your wife and daughters.'

I put the phone down before he'd finished. My voice was nowhere. Afterwards I thought of loads of things I should have said, but at the time I said nothing, just put the phone down and moved into another room. They were going to kill me and Andy and Christy and my dad, and rape Diane and Katy and my mum because we were communists. I didn't really know what 'rape' was but that made it even worse because I knew it was bad and knew I couldn't ask anyone.

I didn't tell Mum that I'd answered the phone but I didn't feel safe after that.

A few days later the lads came round to stay in the front bedroom and Andy and me had to move in with Diane and Katy.

About this time I found a double-barrelled shotgun behind some coats in the wardrobe in my old bedroom. It was dead cold and heavy. I picked it up and weighed it in my arms, then tried to aim it out of the window, looking down onto the road out of the front of the house, but it was so heavy that I couldn't keep it still.

I looked at the triggers for ages, trying to resist pulling one of them. My fingers pressed lightly and then quite hard. It was really quiet in the house and my finger started to itch like mad and I wanted to scratch it on the trigger. I put the shotgun back in the wardrobe and went downstairs to ask Mum about it: 'Mum? Why have we got a gun in the wardrobe?'

She flew into a rage. She and Dad had a big row about it when he came home that night and then he moved it. But the lads stayed in the room. They had pickaxe handles and I just knew they had the shotgun somewhere.

It was like being in a Western waiting for the baddies to come and knowing that someone was going to get it. I wanted them to shoot the fascists so there was blood and bone all over the driveway, and I wanted to watch it.

Mum took all us kids to stay with Bob on his farm. She said it was 'just for a while'.

Uncle Bob's knuckles

Bob was a building worker like Dad but he was also a bit of a farmer. He wasn't our real uncle, we just called him that because he was dad's mate. He was divorced and his two kids lived with his ex-wife. He had a place out by Abergele and the old store room had been changed into a bedroom for us.

Tony and Jeff came to visit a couple of times and we used to go out through the fields and climb trees to get the crows' eggs and blow them and make a collection. Crows were bad because they pecked out the eyes of the newborn lambs. You had to hate crows. You had to throw stones at them.

You could also find loads of dead things in the fields. You could tell when something was dead even before you found it because of the smell. Mostly the dead things were newborn lambs with their eyes pecked out and their bellies ripped open. They were always stiff and you didn't really want to touch them.

Bob was a wide man with big hands but he wasn't very tall. I was nearly as tall as him and I was only eleven. In the beginning he was quite friendly, and he'd call me Nicky, but when Dad had to go away for meetings and things he used to get a bit mean. Then he'd call me a 'dozy bastard'.

Bob did things like this: he'd make a fist with the middle knuckle sticking out and he'd ram it into the top of my head if I did something wrong. I'd never lived on a farm before so I did a lot of things wrong. Sometimes he'd use his special fist to give me a dead arm.

He gave me raw black pudding once because he thought I wouldn't eat it and he could laugh at me, but I did eat it. It was cold clotted black blood with bits of fat. I pretended that I liked it just so he wouldn't laugh and all the time it tasted like swallowing your own nosebleed.

Once he grabbed a sheep from the pen and dragged it by the back legs to the wire washing-line that was strung across the yard. It banged its chin on the concrete and called out to its friends, but Bob just booted it in the ribs and told it to shut up.

Then some other men lifted it up and he tied its back legs to the washing-line. Then he told me to bring the wheelbarrow and hold it under the sheep. The sheep's eyes were wild by now and it was thrashing about on the line.

Bob took a big knife and stuck it deep into the sheep's crotch and sawed the blade all the way down to the sheep's throat. 'Hold still, you dozy bastard!' he said to me.

My hands turning white on the handles of the wheelbarrow while all the guts flopped into it.

It was like watching a murder and you could see the steam coming out of the sheep's insides even after it had stopped bleating and twitching.

Another time he dragged me out of bed in the middle of the night and told me to put a coat on. We went out to the pig-sty.

There was a pig lying on her back and she was grunting and moaning. You had to be careful of pigs because if they bit you they wouldn't let go. They could take your leg off.

This pig was under a big lamp with a hot globe and it was bright and warm and cosy. The pig was lying on straw and she was breathing as though she'd just run all round the farm.

Bob told me to stick my hand up her fanny.

I just looked at him. I didn't want to do that. He shouted at me then and said I had to feel for a piglet, grab it by the snout and pull it out, otherwise they'd all die in there.

This was another test. I had to cover my hand and arm in some sticky greasy stuff and then I went in.

It was long and wet and warm and slimy inside, but as I went deeper in it wasn't so bad. Then I felt this little snout. I told Bob and he said, 'Good, now hold on to it and pull it out.'

I pulled it back down the passage and it just popped out with a wet plop. It was covered in pale blue-green slime like wet plastic and the pig grunted and turned round to look at me. The piglet went round to her and she licked it clean and I went back inside for the others.

That night I delivered the first three piglets, and the remaining nine came out by themselves. I felt fantastic. I watched them for ages snuffling at the teats and even Bob said, 'Well done, Nicky.'

I wanted to tell my dad, but he wasn't there. He was back in Prestatyn guarding the house and waiting for the fascists.

Telling tales

Sometimes when we all had to go to bed early because Mum and Bob wanted to watch telly on their own, we couldn't sleep.

I didn't want to go to sleep because of the dreams. They'd tie up Mum and Dad and Diane and Andy and Katy and Christy and they'd tie me to a chair and ask me which one they should kill first. Other times they'd just torture me to see how much I loved my family. The longer I could take the torture the more of them could live. They'd torture me and torture me and torture me till my flesh was hanging off and my blood was deep on the floor and even though I couldn't feel anything I'd get so scared that I'd give in and they'd laugh and call me a coward and go off to kill my family. It went on for ages.

Instead of sleeping I'd get Diane, Andy, Katy and Christy to sit round on the floor and I would tell them stories. It was dead easy. You could make up anything so long as somebody farted or burped or went to the toilet and then they'd all giggle and say, 'Another, tell another one!'

There were no street lights to take away the darkness and outside you knew there were crows pecking out lambs' eyes.

You'd spend hours listening to everyone breathing and the little sounds of people talking and kissing and shouting and fighting and driving cars in the lounge and you couldn't tell what was real.

Bingo

We were told not to go to Rhyl, which was a big tourist town on the coast, bigger even than Prestatyn, with loads of rides and sweet shops. We'd been there a few times with Mum and Dad.

We were allowed to go through the fields around Bob's farm, but we weren't allowed to go to Rhyl. One day me and Andy worked it out: if we were away the whole day in the fields, how would they know where we were?

We got some money from Mum's purse and set off for the bright lights and the fairgrounds of Rhyl.

We had to hitch-hike but we got lifts easy, and were strolling down the busy pavements by lunchtime. We saw girls wearing 'kiss me quick' plastic bowler hats and T-shirts, giggling as they walked past young men wearing the same. The men shouted in high spirits and carried cans or plastic beakers of beer. The shops were wide open onto the pavement facing the grey sea. You could stop at any of them and look through funny postcards about nudist colonies, then steal some. There were loads and loads of fish and chips shops, too, and we got a whole packet of chips each with extra salt and vinegar. We had about a pound between us so we had to go easy to make it last. There was no way we could even think of going on the Big Dipper in the fairground, but we got plenty of other stuff.

When it started getting late we had to spend the rest of the money and go home. We came across a bingo hall, which I knew about because our nan used to play it. The sign outside said 'Everyone's a winner!' so we went in.

We bought a card and the man started picking numbered ping-pong balls out of the see-through barrel where they were being blown around all over the place. It was dark and warm inside the bingo hall, and it was full of old people smoking cigarettes and staring at their cards.

I thought because we were kids they might let us win. It started off and it went dead fast. You had to look over your whole card all at once and find the number and mark it off, and as soon as you had a line or a row you had to shout 'house'.

I won! I could see it there, a whole line, but I felt shy about shouting 'house' and stopping the game for everyone else. Then Andy nudged me and pointed at the card and I didn't want him to know I was scared so I called out, 'Er … house!'

We had to go to the prize-giving booth and choose our prize. There was no contest; it was a stupid-looking teddy bear, a pair of bright-red edible knickers, or a thick watch with a purple face. I chose the watch. The man set the time and I strapped it to my wrist, looked at the face, then realised to my horror that it was nearly four o'clock.

We ran through the promenade to get to the main road back to Bob's farm, then started hitching but no one stopped. We had to walk. And walk. And walk. We didn't know any short cuts. We kept looking at the watch and it kept getting later and later. We got scared and started making up stories about what had happened. We were going to say we were in a faraway field and we found this watch and then we got lost.

We got onto the long road leading to Bob's farm and a car came up behind us and screeched to a halt. It was Bob. He got out of the car dead fast and made his special fist with his sticking-out knuckle and punched me on the top of the head. At least he let me keep the watch.

The next day Dad came to the farm and we had to pack all our things into the big green suitcase. We were going back home at last.

Plain clothes

It was Valentine's Day 1973 and Dad made us supper because Mum was away in Chester playing bingo with Nan and Aunty Gill. Out of the quiet darkness there was a heavy knock at the front door. We all looked up from the telly for a moment and

Dad looked at me. He was going to tell me to go and answer the door and so I started shifting my weight but then he thought better of it. It wasn't a good idea for any of us kids to answer the front door or even the telephone any more, just in case.

He stepped out of the room and I heard him open the front door. I went to the doorway and looked down the corridor and saw two men in big coats silhouetted against the street light with the mountain at their backs and the occasional car headlight passing behind them. They were filling the doorway and talking to my dad.

'You're joking, aren't you?'

'No. You're under arrest.'

Dad let them in and told them to wait in the sitting room while he made a phone call. They said they'd be fine in the hallway and watched him make his call.

He called Uncle Bob and asked him to come and watch us kids. I couldn't hear everything he said but I could see the two men tapping their gloves against the palm of their hands and looking around the hallway as if for clues.

Dad raised his eyebrows and hooked his finger at me. I ran to him and listened to what he had to say.

'I've got to go out for a bit,' he said to me. 'Bob's coming round to look after you till your mum gets home. Keep the kids in order and don't act the goat.'

'Where are you going?'

'Don't worry about it. It's all a mistake, that's all.'

'Is it because of the food in the freezer?'

He just laughed and ruffled my hair.

Uncle Bob arrived too soon and my dad went out of the house with the two men. Bob was nervous and to hide it he kept smiling all the time and asking if we were all right. He even made a cup of tea for me. I burned my lips on it because it was hot, but I wanted to drink it instead of talking to him.

Later Mum came in and she moved fast. Her voice was high and Bob tried to calm her down. She sent me upstairs with the other kids so they could talk.

Later she came up and started packing the big green suitcase and told me we were going to stay at Bob's place again. I wanted to wait till Dad came home, but she told me not to worry.

Prison

Glan Gerrionedd

The Trial

Cooking at Gerrionedd is not easy. The kitchen is dark and musky, and there are very few pans. Dad can't stomach rich food, so everything has to be bland and easy to swallow. I revert to a student menu of various types of canned mulch, which he seems to like – tinned sardines with tinned lentils mashed up with tinned tomatoes with potatoes on the side.

After lunch on the second day in the farmhouse I ask him about being sent down.

It was 19 December 1973 and nobody thought Dad, Macky Jones and Ricky Tomlinson were really going to be sentenced to prison. The jury members were in intense debate and only reached a majority decision because they were convinced that there would be fines but no imprisonments. So when Macky got nine months, Ricky two years and my dad three years nobody could believe it.

The foreman of the jury left the courtroom shouting, 'Disgusting, it's disgusting' and he was quickly followed by another jury member who slammed the gate of the jury box as he left the courtroom.

'What did you think?' I ask my father now, fifteen years later. He's just taken his pills so he's feeling all right.

'I thought, "Right then, here we go, let's get stuck in right away," and I started planning the campaign with Ricky. We said straight off there was no way we were accepting a guilty verdict and we'd take them on. Our briefs told us early on that if we pleaded guilty there was a deal on the table to give us fines of fifty quid each which the union agreed to pay. Me and Ricky said you're not on. So when they said guilty I still thought there'd be fines and we'd agreed that we'd refuse to pay anyway and do a bit of bird for contempt of court.'

'Did you think about us kids at all, and Mum?'

'Behave yourself! Of course I did. I saw your mum in the gallery before we got sent down.'

He picks up the poker and stabs the logs in the fire, sending sparks scuppering up the chimney. I watch him stretch forward to reach a log that I've set near the grate to dry. He winces with the effort but it remains just out of reach.

I encourage him. 'Get your fat arse off the chair and you'll get the log.'

'Cheeky bastard!' He drops the poker in the grate and leans back gingerly. 'What is this crap you're feeding me?'

The next day is a fine sunny morning. I look out of the window from my bedroom and listen to my dad moving around downstairs making tea. There is no wind and the lake is like dark glass, sombrely reflecting the far mountainside. I think it would be a good idea to go for a drive.

Downstairs Dad is sitting in what has already become 'his' armchair. He is wrapped in his big anorak, cradling a mug of tea and nibbling at a honey sandwich. There is another mug of tea on the log footstool and I fall into the other chair before taking up my own lukewarm cuppa.

Dad raises his greying eyebrows at me in mock reproach. 'What time do you call this?'

I snigger like an adolescent. I am actually enjoying this time with my dad and I think he is, too. His illness is still only in its middle stages and so there are often whole hours where he resembles the man I knew as a kid.

'Fancy shooting out for a pint later?'

'If you like.'

We set off in my old Beetle, driving slowly through the country lanes that lead from the lakeside to the nearest main road, with me stopping to let him out to open and close the many farm gates. I could go the other way around the lake where there are no gates but I like watching him get in and out of the car, cursing each gate.

When we finally hit the main road it is downhill all the way into Llanwrst. But as we approach the town he is consumed by an attack. His body stiffens and, to make matters worse, he needs to pee.

He mumbles as we cross the bridge over the river. Ignoring his pleas to stop, I tell him we'll soon be at the pub. He groans loudly with the threat of anger and frustration in what is left of his voice.

'Gonna piss my pants!'

'We're nearly there.'

We drive around the busy streets of the small town looking for an appropriate drinking hole. His pleas become more and more insistent with his ever-fading voice until he stops abruptly and his face slackens into a mischievous grin. 'There you go, you bastard.'

Glancing over, I see the darkening spread over his crotch and instantly we are both laughing.

I make him sit in it while I pick up some take-outs from the local off-licence and then drive him back to the farmhouse doing all the gates myself. We share abuse all the way.

We have to cut our own firewood and it is easier doing this with the old rusted but sharpened double-handed saw so I get my dad to lend a hand. His pills have kicked in and he's 'come round' again.

The sawhorse is out in a little yard next to the back kitchen – a sort of walk-in scullery added on to the house with a sink and an ancient bottled gas cooker. I set a kettle on the stove for tea after we've finished.

The yard is in the crook of the house. The whiff of wood-smoke floats over the roof. The earth around us is soft underfoot from rain and fallen leaves, and all we can hear is the birds prattling and the occasional sheep bleating on the hills, muffled by the trees.

Placing a log on the sawhorse, we each take an end of the old saw and try to set up a rhythm.

'Was it really conspiracy to cause affray, Dad?'

He levels a gaze at me, measuring his response and then he kicks off.

'The bosses had a blacklist of unionists to make sure none of us could get work,' he says. 'They were running sites with non-union labour with no safety conditions. There were hundreds of fatal accidents a year. A building worker died for every day of the year. What we were trying to do was give the lads the confidence to get behind us and fight for decent wages and conditions. You don't do that by intimidation, do you?'

'Suppose not.'

'And I tell you what – I never went to picket a site where there weren't coppers watching everything. At Shrewsbury the chief constable shook my hand and congratulated me on the conduct of the pickets, for Christ's sake. It was months after the strike that they worked out their charges and made their arrests. On what charges? Not a single specific charge of intimidation or violence or even damage to property against any one of us stood up in court, just conspiracy and protection of property, a blanket charge from an old law that hadn't been used for nearly a hundred years. The whole thing could have been dealt with under the Industrial Relations Act and they went criminal instead. It was a set-up from the word go.'

Though he hasn't moved the saw blade an inch, I can see his grip on the handle turning his knuckles white. His hands are shaking. His legs are shaking and his knees are buckling under his weight. His head starts to nod in tiny, uncontrollable jerks and his mouth has fallen open. He's going into 'bulk'. This is the term he coined, and that we have all come to use when he's suffering an attack of Parkinson's. He is hunching over, collapsing into himself.

'I hope you're not going into bulk now because I'm not doing this log on my own,' I say, trying to lighten the moment.

He barks a single breathless laugh. But the look in his eye makes me falter.

'Just ease your grip on that handle, Dad. It's all right. Take it easy. Breathe.'

He looks down and gazes at his hands on the saw as if they are someone else's. He lets out a low, long groan and I know he's gone. I move round to him, unpeel his fingers and place his hands on my forearm.

'It's all right, mate, take it easy, we'll have a sit-down instead, eh? Come on. Move your feet. One at a time.'

It's a familiar routine and one I have grown to hate.

Together we shuffle through to the front room and I lean back to balance his weight and lay him into his armchair with the kettle now whistling for attention in the scullery.

I've sawn a couple of logs and am getting ready to split them when Dad comes rolling outside with that post-'bulk' gait of his. He walks with strides that are too large for his returning sense of balance and so he appears drunk as he rolls from the heel of one foot to the ball of the other until in the space of a few yards he regains balance.

Smiling, he slaps his hands together and grabs the axe. I step aside and roll a cigarette and watch him get his rhythm after a few strokes, happy to see him up and about and working his body.

I press him on a subject that has long been on my mind. After Ricky and Dad refused to do prison work on their first day inside they split them at the end of the first week. Dad was moved to eight different prisons in the next five weeks.

'What was that all about?' I ask him now.

He lets the axe fall into the log. 'They moved me all the time. Even in a prison they'd come and move me to a different cell whenever they felt like it. It was all part of not letting me settle down and get the measure of the place. I was on edge the whole time, waiting to see what strokes the screws were going to pull next.'

He picks up the axe and slams it into a log, sending splinters all round the small yard.

'I was worried that some of the screws might be lining up to give me a good kicking but something was holding them back. It was all the Labour MPs who kept coming to visit.'

'Where did they move you?'

'Shrewsbury, Bedford, Liverpool, Stafford and then Brixton for the first appeal hearings. Then me and Ricky went on to Wormwood Scrubs together. We were getting loads of mail from all over the country. Workers pledging support and ready for action, but still not a peep out of the leadership. The miners were giving Heath a battering and he announced a general election for the end of February. That's when me and Ricky announced our first hunger strike, demanding political status as victims of the state. Twenty-two days of isolation on nothing but liquids with the screws presenting the most delicious meals every hour of every day. Then Labour got in and we got a telegram from the TUC asking us to start eating because they were confident that all charges would be dropped and we'd all be released.'

'But that didn't happen.'

'No, it didn't. They upheld the charges of conspiracy and unlawful assembly, gave us leave to appeal the charge of affray, but denied bail and shipped us off to Stafford next day.' He splits another log and places the axe carefully against the wall. 'That'll do me.'

He strolls back inside and I pick up the split logs and place them in the crook of my arm, flicking off the woodlice one at a time and watching them fall, dazed and kicking in the dirt.

I've given Dad his pills and pulled a blanket over him. The spasms from another 'bulk' session are calming and he's breathing deeply, dragging gulps of air into his lungs and letting them out slowly as he's been taught to do.

I've positioned myself on a dining chair in the corner of the bedroom and am recounting the tale of the monkey's head on a stick that gave me such a fright. His breathing goes strange and I glance at him worried for a moment before I realise he's laughing. There are tears rolling down his face.

'Another time, I sneaked into the broom cupboard behind the sink and was going to jump out at you,' he says. 'You ran the taps and filled the sink. Then you put your hands into the water. You were so little you couldn't see into the sink. You suddenly pulled your hands out and said, "Fucking hell, that's hot!" I had to bite my tongue to stop from laughing out loud.'

I feel a grin splitting my face. 'You evil bastard. I can't wait to have kids of my own to pull some of those strokes.'

A pale, bony hand emerges shaking from under the blanket to wipe away the tears from his cheeks. I stroll to the window and look over the lake to hide the pride I feel in raising his mirth.

We've finished breakfast the next day but the pills haven't kicked in, and he's still stiff and off balance and needs to go to the toilet.

I pull the covers back and lever him up. His long, white toes curl up tight on the little threadbare rug and there seems to be an acre of blackened floorboards to cross before we reach the door of the bedroom. I grab his hands and try to raise him off the bed, but he groans in pain. We both watch the tiny movements of his toes as he starts to warm them up for action. His alabaster feet gradually come alive. 'Right,' he says, 'let's go.'

I lean back and take his weight and he moans all the way up to nearly upright. Then I stand to the side; take him under the arms as we make slow progress out of the room, along the corridor and into the bathroom. We stop and rest three times on the way.

I place him in front of the toilet bowl. His arms are bent at the elbow with his hands stiff but quaking at his belly. I can see where this is going but I lift the seat before stepping back to let him get on with it.

'Where are you going?'

'I'll wait back here.'

I lean back against the door jamb and inspect the coving between the wall and ceiling with exaggerated attention for a moment.

'Help me.'

I look at the back of his head and see the pink scalp beneath the now wispy waves of silver hair.

'What do you mean?'

'Get me kecks down.'

'You're joking, aren't you?'

'Hurry up.'

'Jesus!'

I push myself away from my leaning position and step up to stand behind him and pull his training pants down without looking. I start to move away again.

'Undies.'

'Come on, Dad, make an effort!'

'Undies!'

I slip my fingers under the elastic waistband and slip his underpants down. Navy blue with a white elasticated waistband. I catch sight of his manhood and quickly look away.

'Is that it? Is that where I came from?'

He laughs.

'No one should have to face something like that first thing in the morning.'

His laughter is hard-earned and with each small convulsion his pee falls into the bowl.

When he has finished I pull up his pants, flush the toilet and lead him out of the bathroom.

We get outside the bedroom and I begin to turn him in that direction.

'Downstairs.'

I carefully lead him downstairs taking most of his weight every careful step of the way. We pull into the sitting room and I lead him over to the chair.

'Floor.'

'What?'

'Put me on the floor.'

I stand in front of him and take his hands firmly in mine. Feeling the bones in his wrist and the pulse of his heart racing, I lean back and lower him to the rug on the floor. He groans all the way down.

'Pillow.'

I take a cushion from one of the armchairs and lift his head to place it. I am surprised to confirm with touch what I have already seen, that his hair is soft and full but grey and thinning now. His head is hot and his neck is stiff. He exhales deeply and starts to straighten his legs, stretching them out towards the fireplace.

'Thanks, Nicky.'

'No problem. But if you want a crap you're on your own.'

Here is the order of events that led to the trial at Shrewsbury in 1973.

The building workers' strike lasted three months and ended in September 1972. It led to a wage increase but no change in safety conditions.

The building federation presented a case for prosecution with evidence of violence and damage to property taken from press cuttings of newspaper accounts.

The investigation started in October 1972 but was dropped after November with no arrests made. It was resurrected in February 1973 and then, five months after the end of the strike, the arrests began.

The first trials were held at Mold Crown Court in June 1973, and even though Dad wasn't on trial, his name was constantly brought up by the prosecution.

During these trials many of the charges were dropped. They simply could not be proved. At the same time, much of the evidence presented by the police was deemed to be inadmissible or inappropriately obtained from witnesses who were said to be exhausted and intimidated at the interviews.

What was established by the prosecution at Mold was that the charges of intimidation and causing affray did not need proof that any blow had been struck, or even that any fighting had taken place. It was enough to produce witnesses who would testify that they were afraid that an assault might take place.

The Shrewsbury Trials began in October 1973. Although no picket had been charged with unlawful assembly at their arrest, this charge was added at Shrewsbury. The prosecution described this charge as being proved at 'any gathering where there is a show of force which if continued could lead to a breach of the peace'.

For the successful prosecution on the other standing charge of conspiracy the judge ruled that 'for conspiracy, they never have to meet and they never have to know each other'. It was enough to show that certain things had happened that had a common pattern.

My father's defence strategy was to explain what he had done at Shrewsbury and why, to attack the political basis of the trial and to turn the charges against the owners of construction companies who flouted the laws on safety and welfare regulations. It was not a successful strategy.

Dereliction

Before Dad went on trial he'd finished fixing the house in Prestatyn and they sold it to buy two cottages that were much cheaper. They were in a village called Henllan near the town of Denbigh and we were all going to live there instead. I thought this was a great idea because then maybe nobody would be able to find us and we'd be safe.

The two cottages had two little front doors next to each other and the first thing Dad did was knock a doorway between the two to make it like one house with two rooms downstairs and a new staircase going up to the two rooms upstairs. Dad said he was even going to make a toilet inside and a separate bathroom.

It was great fun working there with my dad every day. Andy, Christy and I used to go with him and I'd make the tea and hand out the sandwiches when we had a break. Andy and Christy weren't allowed to use any tools because they were too young, but I could, and I learned how to squeeze your thumb really hard after you'd hit it with a hammer by mistake.

One day it was just my dad and me, and we were sitting on a bench made of a scaffold plank between two paint tins outside in the back yard, finishing our tea and looking at the old wooden shed in the corner. We were going to demolish the shed to 'clear the decks' and 'let the dog see the rabbit'. So I picked up the heavy lump hammer and was about to go and start smashing the shed down when Dad told me to 'hold my horses'.

'You can't go tearing into something like that without thinking about it first,' he said. 'Have a good look. See where the main supports are and take them out one at a time. That way the whole thing comes down with minimum effort. Use your loaf before you use your hammer, mate.'

I didn't want to think about it though. I didn't want to think about anything. I just wanted to smash it up.

'Are you going to go to prison, Dad?'

'You never know. Let's get a move on just in case.'

Working with my dad and making our own house together was brilliant, but we couldn't do it all the time and soon we couldn't do it at all because Dad had to go away on trial every day and we had to just move into the house even though it was only half built.

Mum wasn't happy about it either, but then she wasn't happy about anything and I wished she'd stop shouting and crying all the time and just be quiet.

Glad tidings

It was nearly Christmas and the shops were full of it. It was all over the radio and the telly as well. Everywhere you looked out of the windows there were people in posters smiling and gasping with joy.

When Mum wasn't crying or shouting she was smiling. But it was the smile that all adults do when there's something else going on inside, something they don't want you to know but that you know anyway.

All of Dad's mates were smiling too, and in those last few weeks before the trial they kept coming round to our new house to move the furniture around and help with the building and everyone was having a good laugh.

Aunty Gill, Nan and Grandad were doing the same smiles and so I was smiling as well. We were all smiling and talking about Christmas and about how great it was going to be and even Dad joined in and it was like we were all these grinning, smiling happy people who thought that this Christmas was going to be the greatest ever.

So when the day came on 19 December 1973 and Mum came home from the trial with red eyes, her blonde hair looking tired and saggy, and her coat collar up over her face, and she looked at our excited faces, she made that low, terrible sound like an animal and her face fell apart. Then she dropped onto her knees and pulled us all into that terrible embrace of fear and pain and desperation. It was like Christmas had been cancelled for ever.

Then there were men in the house who called themselves 'Dessie's mates' or 'mates of yer dad'. It was dark, cold and wet outside. A weak, naked light bulb hung from the middle of the raw-beamed ceiling of the main downstairs room, and the men had to keep ducking so they didn't bang their heads on it. Someone made tea but nobody drank it.

As they left, one of the men loosened his tie, then leaned down to me and hung it round my neck. He dropped a heavy hand on my shoulder and looked into my face. 'There you go, mate, you're the head of the family now.'

'But why? What did he do?'

'Don't worry, son, he won't be in for long.'

'We'll get him out. You'll see.'

'The unions won't stand for this.'

'Look after your mum.'

When they'd all gone, Mum sent us all up to our bedroom and I lay on my belly staring through the crack in the floorboards to the downstairs room and watched my mum sitting on the edge of her bed with her head in her hands, crying like she was being punched all the time. Diane told me to stop looking.

Christmas Special

There were only two rooms that we could use in the house because the other two were full of building materials. The front door opened straight into the downstairs room and that was used as Mum's bedroom, the sitting room and the kitchen.

There wasn't a proper cooker and you had to fill the sink from a tap that was in the toilet out in the back yard, so Mum said we were going to a hotel for Christmas lunch.

We all dressed in our best clothes, then we got a taxi to the hotel on the high street in Denbigh. It was nice and warm in the restaurant and we had to go up some stairs lined with pictures of posh men and women in red coats with tall black hats sitting on horses with hunting dogs all around them.

The restaurant was small and there were only six tables; ours was the biggest. The other tables just had old people sitting there and we pulled crackers and put our hats on. Mum and me read out the daft jokes and we all swapped our little toys.

There was turkey and everything but we couldn't see the whole bird like we used to at home because it was already cut up in the kitchen and so we only got slices and couldn't ask for a leg.

Mum asked if we could have the wishbone and the waiter cleaned it and brought it to us on a paper napkin and we all put our hands on the bone and wished that Dad would come home soon after the appeal.

After pudding the waiter said our taxi was waiting and Mum paid and we all went home feeling full and a bit sick. We were glad to be back home because we could play with our presents, but it was raining outside and there wasn't enough space in the downstairs room so we had to go up to our bedroom to play.

Andy was in a big sulk because Dad wasn't there and he was trying to play with his toys but couldn't be bothered. Diane was pulling her doll to bits trying to see how the arms and legs worked. Katy was looking through a picture book and Christy was colouring in the floorboards with a felt-tipped pen.

I lay down and watched Mum through the hole in the floorboards. The Queen was talking on the telly but Mum wasn't listening. She was lying on her bed with her arm over her face and her body was shaking.

She was making that big horrible crying noise again and I turned away and tried not to think about it.

Stoked up

One morning Mum was upstairs collecting dirty washing. I was in the downstairs room trying to make a fire to warm us all up just like Tony had taught me. But it kept going out and the kids were making a big racket and Christy kept pestering me to make breakfast. He wouldn't leave me alone and suddenly I lost my temper and turned on him with the coal shovel. I pushed it at him and it caught him on the head just above his eye. I grabbed him hard and hugged the screams out of him. 'I'm sorry, I'm sorry, please don't tell Mum and I'll be your best friend!'

By the time Mum came downstairs Christy had stopped screaming, but he was still bleeding and we all said that he'd tripped and fallen.

Later on I was bringing a bucket of water I'd filled at the outside tap into the house for cooking and I tripped and it went all over the floor and settled in small pools between the slate tiles.

It was like she'd been waiting for it. She shot up. 'We can't live like this!'

'I'm sorry, Mum. I'll clean it up.'

But Mum only told me to look after the kids for a while and dragged her coat on like she was fighting it. Then she went down the road to the phone box. I was going to do potatoes but I did sandwiches instead and Katy got upset because she was looking forward to potatoes. She was at the age when she would say 'why' all the time, no matter what you told her.

'We're having cheese sandwiches instead.'

'Why?'

'Because they're better.'

'Why?'

'Because they're easier.'

'Why?'

'Cos you don't have to cook them!'

'Why?'

It drove me mad.

When Mum got back we all had to pack our things and eat our sandwiches at the same time so we couldn't really enjoy them and then Bob came and he kept his coat on. I knew what that meant. We were leaving.

We drove for quite a long time and my head spun round excitedly when I saw the sign that said 'Croeso y Prestatyn'.

'Are we going to our old house, Mum?'

'No, we're going to another place.'

We pulled into a long dark driveway with a tall dark hedge on one side and a field with caravans on the other. We stopped in the lane and you could see a huge house ahead through the trees. I thought maybe that was where we were going to live.

But no. We were going to live in the caravan park. It was going to be brilliant, like being on holiday the whole time.

Holiday accommodation

I loved living in the caravan. It was like an adventure and meant we would be with our friends, who thought we were never coming back to school.

The caravan had cupboards and a little kitchen with a sink and the tables turned into beds when you needed them to. Outside there was a playground with a climbing frame and swings near the toilets. Because there was nobody staying there at that time of year we had the whole place to ourselves.

We all got these little tins on the end of string and you'd swing them round your head and they'd whistle like birds. You had to swing them faster or slower depending on if you wanted a high- or low-pitched sound. Andy and me would stand outside the caravan for ages swinging our bird-calls, trying to get the blackbirds to answer.

Later we moved into a chalet in the same park. It was made of wood and there was carpet on the floor. The whole place had that special smell when you were cooking, like warm gas in cold air. It was still cold like the caravan but there was an electric fire where you could make toast by holding the bread with a long fork that came free with the chalet.

We used to have Angel Delight nearly every night after supper and Mum let us all call it 'pink poo'. Sometimes she'd say, 'What do you want for dessert?' And we'd all shout, 'Pink poo, pink poo!'

One day we all went out of the park and ran over the scrubby grass that grew out of the sand and into the dunes. Mum told me not to take my bingo watch with me because it would get broken. I said I wouldn't take it but I kept it in my pocket and put it on when she wasn't looking. In the dunes Andy and me played Jack and Joe in a war film and I kept checking my watch so I could 'synchronise' with my men.

I stood at the top of a sand dune and looked out to sea with my arms wide and my mouth open and I swallowed the air because it tasted like the blue skin on the bottom of a fish that sticks to the batter. By the time it was nearly dark there was sand inside my watch and it didn't work properly ever again but I kept it for ages just in case.

I remember being in the washrooms with Mum when she was washing some socks at the basin. I saw one of Dad's razor blades and asked Mum what it was for. She told me not to touch it. We were waiting for Dad to come out on bail for his second appeal and I thought if I just held his razor everything would be all right. So I touched it and sliced off the top of my finger like you do with a boiled egg. It didn't hurt but the blood poured out and Mum threw the bar of soap she was using into the basin and made a big splash and walked out of the bathroom shouting, 'What did I tell you?'

I tried to put the flap of skin back but it just rotted over the next few days, with the sort of smell that you could only get properly if you put your finger up your nose. For ages it was a smooth bit on the top of my finger with no fingerprint. I thought it would be really handy for doing robberies.

Sometimes Bob used to come round to visit in the week and most weekends we had to go to his farm. Mum would talk to him for ages about 'the campaign' and she would get angry because her husband was a building worker and we had to live like gypsies.

Jumble

It seemed as though it stayed cold and wet for a long time that year, and it got dark early all the time. One day after school Mum told me she was going to organise a jumble sale and she needed my help. I loved jumble sales but I wasn't happy when she said how it involved me. But even though I was the head of the family she was still my mum and I had to do as I was told.

She emptied Christy's old pram and told me I had to go to the posh parts of Prestatyn asking for jumble for charity. I spent a whole week going up and down the steep roads pushing that pram, going from door to door saying, 'Excuse me, hello. I'm collecting jumble for charity.'

Some people didn't have any jumble and some people told me to come back tomorrow and I had to try to remember their house but I never could because I didn't have a pen and paper. Old people were the best. They had loads of jumble: comics; food blenders; old coats that smelled like moth balls; and creased fur hats that smelled like the back of Grandad's armchair.

A couple of times strict, angry old men wearing slippers and smoking pipes or cigars would ask me what I was collecting for and I'd say for charity and they'd say what charity and I'd say I didn't know and they'd snuffle down their noses and slam the door. Some of the doors had stained glass and you could see them mumble as they walked back down their hallway and I knew they were right and I was wrong but I thought they should bog off because my mum told me to do this.

Inside some houses you could hear the telly and smell food cooking. You could feel the warmth from inside when they opened their doors and you wondered what it must be like to have all those rooms.

Sometimes I'd wonder if they had kids that went to my school. That was the worst thing – hoping that nobody from school saw me because I knew the charity was really us.

When I got back to the chalet each night Mum got dead excited and we all sat around and emptied the pram and she let us choose the things we wanted. We could have all of the old toys as well as all the comics. Mum went to the launderette and put some of the clothes into the washing machine and days later she'd be wearing some of the stuff and other things would be hanging in our wardrobe. I didn't mind so much once the musty smell was gone.

After about two weeks of doing this Mum made me load up the pram with all the things we didn't need and I had to take it all down to the vicarage and give it to the carpet man.

He pretended not to remember who I was, which was fine with me.

Pike

I dreamed of fish, pike mostly. Pike grew big and their teeth were like busted-up saw-blades pointing inwards so there was no escape. Some people called them the 'freshwater shark'. You could see them in books in the library. These were not the kind of books you'd buy because they cost loads. The only thing you could buy was the *Angling Times*. This had pictures of all sorts of fish but they were mostly strung up and hanging off weighing scales with fat men standing next to them in black and white. They'd lost all their power and they were dead.

The books were special, the words like scripture. You'd read the words and you almost wouldn't need the pictures. My favourite book was all about pike-fishing in winter. There were all these magical landscapes of brown and black grit, and pieces of the frozen ground poking out of the snow like bran flakes in milk. You could hear the stillness in those pictures. You could almost see your breath in front of your face even when you were tucked up reading under the covers with your torch. Sometimes the rivers were ice and you had to break through to get your bait in there. In the books there were small streams with the tall grass all along the edges and they were there in real life, too, if you walked far enough. They were like secrets.

On walks through the fields I would stop and stare into that brown, gurgling water and look for brown trout, almost impossible to see unless you were patient and waited for your hunter's eyes to kick in.

I wanted to fish and got myself some lengths of drain-cleaning poles that Bob brought back from work. I cut notches in the end to tie my line and I made hooks out of safety pins. I never caught anything. I was fishing in the wrong places — ditches and the brackish water where the river met the sea.

When we went to visit Dad in prison, we'd have to sit in the car with Bob or on the train and listen to Mum talk about 'the campaign' for hours and hours. Then once we'd arrived, we'd have to sit in the waiting room, not looking at the other people because they were quite rough and a bit scary, and we couldn't play in case we got dirty. In the beginning, we used to meet

Ricky's wife, Marlene, and their kids. Then they sent Dad and Ricky to different prisons so they couldn't be mates any more.

Then the door would eventually open and we'd hang back for a few minutes while all the other visitors pushed each other to go through to the visiting room.

A quick look around the whole room and then my eyes would prickle and my breath would go funny when I saw my dad standing up at his table with his hulking shoulders and flat-mouthed smile.

Dad mostly spoke to Mum about 'the campaign' rather than to us but once he turned to me.

'How are you, mate?'

'I'm all right. I've got a fishing rod made of drain cleaners.'

'Good on ye.'

Then he turned back to Mum and started talking about the appeal that was coming up. I wanted everyone to go away so me and my dad could talk about fishing, but there was never any time.

Bob-a-job

I wasn't in the Boy Scouts because we couldn't afford the uniform. I really wanted to join though. In some of the comics I read about boys who went to boarding school and lived in dormitories together and had great adventures during the school term, but even more during the holidays. It was like the army but for kids and I thought it must be great, even though I hadn't liked the dormitory at the orphanage.

Some of the lads at school were in the Scouts and they started talking about bob-a-job week. What you did was go round to old people's houses and say, 'Bob-a-job?' Then they'd let you in and you'd have to tidy up the attic or do some weeding in the garden or clean the bins and they'd give you a shilling – sometimes more.

All you had to do was be polite and you could do maybe ten jobs a day! You could make loads. You'd have to give some of it to the Scout leader, but you could keep some of it for yourself. Charlie made sure he had loads of pockets and put one of the coins he was keeping for himself in a separate pocket so the Scoutmaster couldn't hear a clink when you told him that was all the money you'd got.

The only thing was, you had to be in a Scout's uniform. I thought I'd give it a go anyway and I did all right. It was school holidays and I spent every day out there doing jobs. If anyone asked where my Scout uniform was I said it was in the wash.

Not everyone wanted help but some did. I did weeding and cleaning-up and people would give me lemonade and sandwiches as well as money.

A young woman lived in one of these houses. Her husband was away a lot just like my dad and she needed loads of help. First I helped her in the garden and tidied up around the bins, and then I did a bit of painting. She was really nice and kind. Once she asked me to come inside and she gave me black cherries out of a tin smothered in thick cream.

I told Mum all about the young woman and how nice she was and how she wanted me to go and help her every Saturday.

Mum's face went all stiff and she told me I wasn't allowed to go back there again.

'Why not?'

'Don't answer back. I'm your mother and you'll do as I say.'

The next day I went down to that woman's house again, stood on the other side of the road and looked up at her bedroom window. I could see the wood-panelled back of her dressing-table mirror in front of the window and her elbows sticking out either side. I knew she was brushing her hair and that she was lonely. I watched for ages then got nervous in case she saw me and waved at me to come in and help her.

I turned and ran all the way down to the lido by where we used to live and spent the day knocking the cake walk machines in the penny arcade, and collecting pop bottles to get the deposit back.

Hairdo

Mum started getting into 'the occult' in a big way. I didn't really know what it was all about. Mum and her mates would do their horoscopes and Mum would hold their hands and tell them things. I used to have to go with Mum almost everywhere at that time so I saw a lot of the occult world.

They were very keen on the occult in the hairdresser's. They would sit in rows with big metal hats that blew hot air. I had to sit there by the window watching ordinary people go up and down Prestatyn high street. Men never came in, but sometimes they'd look inside and catch my eye and I felt embarrassed.

The smell in the hairdresser's was thick, and you could taste the fine mist in your throat of perfumes, shampoos and hair lacquer. Sometimes you'd hope for someone new to come in just so they would open the door and let some fresh air in. I'd have to read women's magazines because that's all there was. Loads of stories about women getting better. Every magazine was the same. The women would mutter quickly under their breath about how they felt about stuff. They felt a lot of different things.

Once I was flicking through *Titbits* or *Women's Weekly* when Mum turned to me. 'Come on, Nicky, you're next.'

She was pointing at a chair and the hairdresser was smiling down at me. All I could see were her teeth and her shiny eyes and the rest was all just big pink face. All the other women were looking at me from under their big hot hats. I tried to make myself smaller. I closed my mouth tight and hunched my shoulders. 'I don't need a haircut.'

They all laughed. My hair was just right; it was nice and thick, a bit greasy so it stayed down close to my head, and now they were going to make it fluffy like the horrible picture they were showing me!

The hairdresser had thick legs in brown tights so they looked like plastic, a bright yellow apron tied tight around big hips, and massive boobs. The woman's hands were all over my head and the water was trickling down my neck and the scissors were snipping and the woman was sticking her breasts in my face, resting her thigh against my knees and making me hot and embarrassed.

The hairdryer blew into my mouth and my eyes, over and over again, and it was like being car sick. Finally she took off the apron and spun the chair round for me to see in the mirror. My hair was blow-dried. It was the worse thing that could happen. Blow-dried hair was for girls, everyone knew that – everyone except mums and hairdressers.

Now we had to go outside and everyone would look at my stupid perfumed hair. We walked up the high street, past the church on the other side of the road and the spot where a girl from school had touched some electricity cables that had blown down in the storm. She had died right there. I wished I was dead as well.

We went into an antique shop. Mum walked up to a big old woman in a kaftan and they hugged each other. I hated the way Mum hugged people.

'This is my eldest, Nicky.'

I didn't even smile but the woman put her hands on my head and stroked my cheek. 'Oh yes, he's going to be a real lady-killer.'

I wanted to get out of the shop there and then but Mum told me to stay put. They moved through to the back of the shop together and went behind a curtain. I looked through all the shelves of old things for a while and got bored, so I followed them to the back and peeped through a chink in the curtain. It was dark in the back room except for the candles and the burning red eyes of joss sticks. Mum was having her tarot cards read. The old woman was looking serious and their mumblings didn't sound happy. I thought it might have been about me growing up to be a lady-killer but secretly knew it was all about Dad.

When it was over I thought I could go home and hide my hair. But Mum told me she'd got me work for that day that was better than bob-a-job. It was a job at the local newspaper. I thought this sounded all right till I got there. They looked at me, did all that smiling and stroking, then gave me a new school uniform and a pair of shiny shoes.

There was a girl there as well. She was much older than me, maybe fifteen. She was also in a school uniform. When I'd got dressed they made us both stand in a stupid way with one foot sticking out in front of the other. There were white walls and a white floor and big lights.

'I don't want to do this, Mum,' I said, and kept trying to flatten my hair but it kept just springing back up. They pulled at my jacket to make it straight, the tie as well. They were going to take photographs of me looking like a girl and then put it in the paper for the whole world to see. And there was nothing I could do.

They made the girl hold my hand and then they asked me to smile. I couldn't smile but I made the smile shape with my mouth and they seemed happy with that. I looked from Mum to the woman who kept fluffing my hair to the woman behind the camera, and when it was all over I asked Mum where my money was. She just laughed.

Stray

When we went to stay on Bob's farm I'd try not to think about Bob and what mood he might be in, or what he might make me do or what I might do to make him angry. I'd think of the good things instead.

One of the good things was his dog, Stray. He was a Jack Russell and he'd just turned up on the farm years before. Bob had taken him in and he was actually quite good at herding sheep, being a watchdog and eating stuff that was thrown out. He was also great company because you could play with him and make him fetch sticks. He'd come with me and Andy on our long walks through the fields, as we collected and blew crows' eggs.

Stray lived within the farm and Bob told us that we should never take him out of the gate that led onto the road. But I thought it was sad that he had to live like a prisoner and so one day I decided to set him free. Andy and me would take him to see the outside world.

Tying a piece of baling twine around his neck one afternoon I led him out of the gate and along the road. He didn't like the lead because he wasn't used to one and he bucked a bit at first, but soon got used to it when I patted him and shouted at him until he worked out what was good and what was bad.

We walked all the way along the road to the next farm where we bought apples and fresh milk. We kept Stray on the lead the whole time so he didn't run off and 'worry' the sheep, because that's the kind of thing farmers hate and they shoot dogs for doing it. We ate our apples and drank our milk, then walked back to Uncle Bob's farm.

Stray really enjoyed that outing but it was the wrong thing to do. Once he'd got a taste of freedom and all the wonders of the outside world he used to go out by himself. He went out by himself every day for about two weeks until he got run over and killed by a car.

When Bob told us about it I felt really sad, guilty and also scared because I knew I was going to get a beating or at least one of Bob's special knuckles on the head. He was holding a shovel when he told me and I thought he was going to smash me with the shovel but instead he just handed it to me and I flinched. He pointed into the stony field. 'Go and dig a hole and bury him.' He told me that Stray's body was on a shelf behind the pig shed.

Stray's corpse was small and stiff, and there were flies buzzing around it. I didn't want to touch it and decided to go and dig the hole first to give me more time.

I tried to find a spot in the stony field that looked easier to dig than the rest and was near the ditch, away from where the plough went. Then I dug until the hole was wide and deep enough.

Back outside the pig shed, I placed the wheelbarrow beneath the shelf, then I got a fence post and prised Stray's body off the shelf until he fell into the wheelbarrow. It tipped over when Stray landed and a cloud of flies flew up. I had to keep my mouth shut and my eyes half closed so they couldn't get inside me and lay maggots. Then I quickly pushed him back into the wheelbarrow with my boot.

Humming a tune all the way to the hole to keep me from running away from the task, I poured the body into the hole, pressed it into place with the shovel and quickly covered it up.

When it was done, all the flies had gone off looking for

something else that was dead and rotting. I sat down on Stony Field and said a prayer. I wasn't really praying to God with the beard but just said I was really sorry about introducing Stray to the outside world.

Looking up, I saw Bob staring at me from the fence nearby and was embarrassed because he might have seen me crying. But he said something else. 'You know your dad's coming out next week, do you?'

'No! For ever?'

'Well, I don't know about that – we'll have to see.'

Glan Gerrionedd

Fighting and Appealing

I've set up a camping chair for Dad outside by the lake so he can read the news. He cracks open the paper and begins his usual routine: 'Fucking hell! ... Look at this! ... Jesus Christ! ... Gobshites!'

I look over the lake so he can't see me laughing. I bought him a right-wing tabloid on purpose. Then there's a silence behind me. I turn to see Dad smirking at the newspaper.

'What's that, Dad?'

'Horoscope.'

'What's it say?'

'Same old rubbish. I'm just remembering. When I was inside I used to read my stars. Once when I'd been in solitary for about five months, I read, "You should take this opportunity to get out more."'

It's raining outside in that Welsh way, as though it could be pouring down all over the world. The water slips down the windowpanes, and is whipped into zigzags by the wind. The lake is kicking up a fuss with mean little waves chopping their way slantwise across to the far shore. There's a stew on the cooker bubbling away in a beat-up pan; until it's time to eat there's nothing to do.

Dad yawns and runs his fingers through his hair. Suddenly there's a sense of quiet. I glance out of the window. The rain's stopped.

'Do you want to get out for a bit of air?'

He doesn't answer, just swings himself out of the chair and starts pulling on his boots.

It's soft underfoot and quiet as we walk up the hill. It's as if the birds and the sheep are listening to how far we'll get. It isn't very far but when we stop we can see over the roof of the farmhouse to the far mountain range. It looks good and we watch in silence as our breath settles.

Dad wobbles ever so slightly as he tries to get a good balance. He leans against the rain-darkened trunk of a pine tree and stuffs his hands in the pockets of his anorak. I roll up a cigarette and light it. The light-blue smoke climbs lazily upwards into the deep black branches above me.

I watch his toes wriggling and flexing under the leather of his boots. They are old boots of mine that are too small for me now; I've grown bigger than him over the years.

They were finally let out on bail pending their appeal on the affray charge in June 1974. For the eight weeks of the five months they were out on bail, Dad and Ricky got jobs on a site in Liverpool – not because their unions pulled any strings, but because one of their mates, Tony Ledgerton, was a shop steward on the site and he put them at the front of the queue for work. Tony held a meeting with all the lads on the site, as well as many others who were lining up to get work there, and they all voted to give Dad and Ricky a start. Their lawyers said it would give them a better chance of a positive hearing at the appeal.

The bosses didn't want to take them on but they dropped the issue when the site threatened to go on strike otherwise.

With the Labour Party in power and hundreds of thousands of workers up and down the country marching and lobbying, and the Trades Councils passing resolutions for their release, most people thought the appeal was going to go well.

But the different attitudes of workers and the unions representing them soon became clear.

The building unions UCATT and TGWU condemned the Shrewsbury Pickets as violent – even though not a single act of violence was ever proved – and merely complained about the harshness of the sentences.

In January 1974 London building workers had lobbied the law courts around the first appeals. Further demonstrations were organised in Glasgow and London. Work stopped in protest on twenty-five Manchester building sites. Thousands of workers from different industries marched on the day of the first appeal hearings, stoppages were organised in factories in Dundee, and North Wales building workers stopped work for the day.

In October the decision on the second appeal was announced. The judges quashed the affray charge but held up the charges of conspiracy and unlawful assembly and, referring to recent picketing by lorry drivers in Hull, stated that 'if the court sets aside these sentences it will undo all the good work that has been achieved'.

From inside their cells at Wormwood Scrubs Dad and Ricky could hear the shouts of angry workers at the prison gates. The next morning they were moved out to a remote prison in Sudbury, far from the industrial centres of a gathering storm of protests.

It's started raining again and we've been standing listening to water fall through the branches for about twenty minutes.

'I enjoy these little chats, don't you?' I say.

Dad laughs and rolls back on the balls of his feet. He pushes his tongue over his bottom front teeth and looks at me straight in the eye with a thin smile cracking the features of a grey but closely shaved face. 'Aye.'

Inside out

We were living in the caravan park when Dad came home on bail. He walked down the narrow path to our chalet and the sun was breaking through the high hedge, casting light and shade over his face, and he was smiling and Katy and Christopher jumped into his arms and he lifted them up as he hugged Mum, and Diane ran to join in and Andy and me stood around, trying to get close but not wanting to show it.

We had a big cake and some tea in the pot and we all sat around, trying to catch his eye, and Mum kept holding his hand. You could see they couldn't wait for us to go to bed so they could be together. He said the charges against him were political and wouldn't stand up to the appeal.

Then he took a big sip of tea and looked around the chalet. 'Christ Almighty, it's like the Swiss Family Robinson in here!'

We all laughed even though the smaller kids didn't know what he meant.

Later we took him outside and down the little path through the secret gate to the sand dunes, and he and Mum walked along the shore holding hands, the kids buzzing around them both. I hung back and watched and it looked just like when we had first moved to Prestatyn – not so long ago really – except this time I didn't ask him how cold he thought the sea was.

Dropping the hat

We all thought Dad would be with us when he came out but I wasn't really surprised when he had to go away loads for meetings and sometimes even to work. Sometimes at night, when he was home, I could hear him and Mum talking about 'the defence committee' and Dad said they were rubbish.

One night we came back from a visit to Bob's farm. Dad and Bob had been arguing and Mum was trying to stand up for Bob because he was a member of the defence committee. She was getting on my nerves. You could tell Bob was embarrassed though.

'The committee wasn't set up to build people's houses.'

'It's a disgrace. You've got this lot living like bleeding refugees and there's a thousand building workers that'd finish the Henllan house at the drop of a hat if you asked them.'

'I agree, Des, and I've asked the committee and got no joy. That's why I've been working on the house on my own at the weekends – but there's only so much I can do.'

On the drive home Mum tells him how great Bob is and how hard he's been working, and Dad goes all quiet because he's not allowed to swear in front of us kids and all he wants to do is swear.

We pull into the big dark driveway of the caravan park and stop behind Bob's car.

Dad rips open the car door and gets out quickly. Bob is standing by his car now and the two of them start shouting at each other. Dad keeps pointing back at us in the car and Bob puts his hands up with his palms open, trying to calm him down.

My heart was racing. I thought Dad was going to deck him. I didn't know why but I really wanted this to happen. I remembered the feel of Bob's knuckles on my head and wanted him to feel my dad's knuckles in his face. I kept wishing he'd stop arguing and just use his fists so I could watch Bob fall.

But just when it looked like it was going to happen, Mum got out of the car and separated them. Mum really liked Bob.

Split cane

On my thirteenth birthday Dad crept into our bedroom and tweaked my toe like he always did to wake me up: 'Come on you, lazy bleeder, up you get!'

I started getting dressed and only then remembered what day it was. It was still very early, only just light, and I went through to the kitchen wondering what I'd get this year.

Dad was sitting at the table with two mugs of tea and he watched me wander through from the bedroom with a smile on his face. He pushed the mug across the table to me. 'There's your tea. And oh aye, this is for you an' all.'

It was a split-cane fishing rod, unwrapped but with the three sections tied together by a piece of string.

'Better than those old drain rods you've been using, eh?'

Split cane was a bit old-fashioned by then, all the best rods were fibreglass, but I didn't complain. I couldn't believe he'd remembered. I only mentioned it once in the prison.

'Thanks, Dad, it's brilliant.' I couldn't wait for my next chance to fish.

'Well, you'll have plenty of time to fish in those rivers around Henllan. But first we've got to get the house in order. Sup up and let's get a move on.'

Loggerheads

We left the chalet and moved into a rented house 20 miles away. It was on the main road of a small Welsh town called Holywell. I had to go to a new school for a while. The only good thing about this school was that all the girls thought I was 'lovely' because I was shy and scared. I was shy because I didn't know anyone and I was scared because of Arthur Inskip.

Arthur Inskip didn't like me because I was a new boy and because the girls liked me. He was only a little lad but he was tough and he was angry. The first week, during every break, he'd push me down the hill past the playground onto the grass where he could stand higher up on the slope and kick and punch me.

I didn't want to fight him for all sorts of reasons. Everyone either liked Arthur or they were scared of him, so if you had a fight with Arthur you had a fight with the whole school. I just wanted to fit in and find my place. Again.

But you couldn't just let someone smack you around every break-time. I'd spend all the lessons thinking about how to get

Arthur to like me and not beat me up when the bell went.

Mum realised that I wasn't happy at the new school and so, typically, she made a big decision – no more school. I didn't go to school until we left Holywell months later.

When I wasn't working with Dad on the house in Henllan because he was working in Liverpool I went with Mum. Most of the time we went for rides on buses. We went all over North Wales to places like Conwy, Betws-y-Coed, Blaenae Ffestinniog, Ruddlan, St Asaph and even Rhyl. We'd go into shops to look at things and into tea shops and eat scones and cream. We'd sit at the back of the nearly empty bus and watch grey people with cloudy faces smoke. The bus smelled like a lift and when it stopped you could hear the brakes hiss and smell the diesel. I'd look out of the windows and see the farms and the woods when I wasn't talking to Mum and when we nearly got where we were going I'd hold her make-up bag while she 'put her face on'. It wasn't embarrassing because nobody looked at us.

One time we came down a hill and there was a sign for the town called Loggerheads. I knew that Loggerheads was a real word but wasn't sure what it meant till Mum told me. We tried to imagine why the people decided to call their town Loggerheads. We thought maybe there were two very important people who established the town and they wanted to call it different names and there was a big battle and lots of trouble and eventually the town's people decided to call it Loggerheads because the big knobs couldn't agree on a proper name.

We went to an auction there. It was in large warehouse at the back of a tiny little shop and everyone had to stand very close to each other. I'd saved up 50p. Mum and me were by the door when the bidding started. I had my eye on a pink glass ring-cleaner that I wanted to buy for Mum and had to wait for ages before I could bid for it. It was like a little ashtray with a tiny pole growing out of the middle like a finger. Mum said that what you did was put washing-up liquid in the bowl and wash your rings and then hang them on the glass finger to dry.

Mum had lots of rings and I had 50p. I bid 10p at a time against a man until I got to 50p and the man got it for 60p. My heart was beating dead fast and I hated him. I was only a kid and he knew I wanted it. It seemed unfair. Mum told me not to worry, it was the thought that counted, and she kissed me on the head.

Mum got some more horse-brasses for her collection and later we went to a tea shop in Loggerheads and had tea and cakes looking out of the window at the river.

Later I bought myself a Lone Ranger with a hole in his bum and a horse called Silver with a plastic bit sticking up out of his saddle so you could stick it up the Lone Ranger's bum so that he could ride without falling off.

I didn't mind going around with Mum but I preferred doing real work with my dad.

Entertaining the shovel

Mum couldn't keep me out of school for ever because some people called Social Services said I had to go back. Mum called them the SS just like the worst ones in the German army who wore black uniforms.

But at last it was the school holidays and that meant that I could go with Dad to our house in Henllan every day to 'crack on with the renovations'. This time it wasn't just my dad and me though, there were loads of lads who came to help, including Ricky, and the place started to take shape. Even though Ricky was really a plasterer, he'd get stuck into doing all sorts of other things as well, like a bit of joinery and some labouring.

My job was to make tea and sandwiches and cement, carry materials and tool bags, and select and pass out the right tools to the right men.

They used to have a lot of laughs and swear at each other but in a nice way, and the big thing was not to cry if you got hurt when you missed a nail and hit your thumb with a hammer, or dropped a beam on your foot.

One day Ricky was upstairs laying a new floor in what was going to be my bedroom. You could hear him up there dragging sheets of chipboard into place and singing out loud. He was always singing and sometimes he'd make banjo sounds with his mouth as well. Then suddenly there was a short sharp scraping sound and a bang followed by a big thump that shook the whole house, then silence.

Dad called up to Ricky but there was no answer so he ran upstairs to see what was going on. He found Ricky straddling one of the floor beams with his legs dangling down either side. He had his whole fist in his mouth and he was biting his knuckles with tears in his eyes. 'Me bollocks!' he said through his fist.

Dad burst out laughing and all the other lads came up and laughed, but Ricky had to go home for the day.

Mixing up the concrete and cement for the floors and the

walls was hard work. One time I was outside the front door doing another mix and all the men were standing around drinking tea and watching me, so I worked as hard as I could. Bob was smiling because he could see I was getting tired. 'I couldn't entertain a shovel these days,' he said.

All the other men agreed that mixing pug was work for younger blokes.

I threw the shovel into the pile of cement. 'Fuck off, the lot of you!'

They roared with laughter and slapped me on the back as I strode into the kitchen to make myself a cup of tea.

I was standing over the kettle, listening to them all filling the wheelbarrow and laughing.

'He's got his dad's spirit right enough,' someone said.

The kettle started steaming and I saw the smile spread over my reflected face. I thought I might as well make tea for everyone.

Most days there was a police car parked just up the road from our house, but we ignored it.

The house was nearly finished in next to no time and we all moved in. Andy and me shared a room, Diane and Katy shared a room with Christy, and Mum and Dad had their own bedroom. We had a toilet inside and a separate bathroom, and downstairs there was a sitting room, a dining room and a kitchen.

The outside toilet was now used to store tools and other things that we wouldn't need any more. The old wooden shed was gone and so we had a back yard to play in, as well as hills, woods and fish-filled rivers.

We all had to pack our own things in boxes so the movers

could stack them all in the back of a big truck that was parked outside on the main road.

Mini-getaway

We'd been living in Henllan for a few weeks and I'd been down to explore bits of the river a few times with my fishing rod but nothing had ever happened to test the line. My first real fishing trip was a week or so later when the family all went to stay in a hotel in Llangollen for the weekend. We had to go there because Mum and Dad hadn't seen enough of each other because Dad was always away and soon his appeal was coming and 'it could go either way'.

As soon as we'd been given our rooms I took my fishing rod, tackled up and went out onto the balcony. Our room was on the first floor and there was a 20-foot drop straight down to a tributary of the River Dee. The rest of the river went around the other side of the hotel to where Mum and Dad were staying.

Warning Andy not to tell anyone, I put my safety-pin hook on the end of my real fishing line and squeezed a bit of bread on the end. Slowly I lowered the bait into the river, down to a gap in the long reeds. The rod was long enough to stretch right across the narrow walkway in front of the ground-floor rooms so no residents could see what I was doing and report me for high-rise fishing.

The hook was in the water for about a minute before I got a bite. It was like nothing I'd expected. It felt as though a man was trying to snap my line. I pulled up quick as a flash and Andy shouted because down there on the end of my line was this snake, writhing in the air. An eel!

Then my rod splintered and snapped and the eel splashed back into the river and wriggled off the hook.

The rest of the holiday was really, really boring after that. It was all museums and ice cream and being polite at mealtimes.

Hound dog

Mum and Dad were very tense with each other at that time. Sometimes the new house was dead quiet because almost no cars passed by our front door and all you could hear were the birds singing in the cow field opposite near the vicarage. You could even hear the toilet cistern filling up, the geyser getting warm and the pipes creaking.

So when Mum and Dad had a row it was dead easy to hear everything they said. It was always about 'the case' and 'the appeal' and 'the campaign'. They used to tell us to go and watch telly in the front room but no matter what was on or how loud it was, you could always hear them shouting.

Then we got a dog, a Labrador called Bruce, and they'd tell us to go and take him for a walk. Once we all went out and walked up the street to the football field and played with Bruce for as long as we could. When we got bored we went back home. Even from up the road we could hear that they'd stopped shouting. We got closer to the house and looked through the window and watched for a moment and then opened the front door and watched even more.

Dad was throwing Mum around the kitchen and as she was about to fall he'd catch her and drag her back to him and she'd twirl around his back with her feet off the ground and come back to his front to land and they'd do it all over again with Elvis Presley singing loudly out of the radio. Then they stopped and laughed and fell into each other's arms and we all clapped.

Porridge

Dad and me used to watch *Porridge* when he was out on bail. We'd sit together in the same room but on different chairs and every now and then we'd laugh. Sometimes Mum or the other kids would come in and watch as well, but they didn't enjoy it as much as Dad and me.

Porridge was all about two blokes who shared the same cell in prison and there was something quite comforting about that because it made prison seem not so scary.

It was funny, but it also had a message, which was that older people knew more about the world than younger people so it was their job to look after the youth. Youth could go astray, and only experience could help get it back on track.

But the best bits were when it showed that youth could be right and experience could be wrong. I liked it when that happened because Fletch was like Godber's dad and I thought that if I was in prison with my dad we'd have a good laugh.

Nobody thought Dad was going back to prison. Everybody thought he was going to win his appeal.

Parting gift

Dad was sorry my split-cane fishing rod had snapped so soon and so he took me to get another rod from Woolworths. It was made out of fibreglass and it could take a fish up to 10lb. You could prove it, too. The rod would bend nearly in half without breaking.

In the *Angling Times* you'd see that the best reels you could get were Shakespeare. Mine was a Rhino-reel and it came with the rod in the same packet. But because it was new I thought it would be easy to swap for a Shakespeare at school.

I had an old tool bag that Dad had given to keep my fishing rod and tackle in. I had lead weights that you had to press onto the line without breaking it, lots of different-sized hooks, some old margarine tubs for bait and even a couple of spinners.

Down by the river where we used to go you could see other people's lines and floats sometimes snagged out by the rocks and even up in the branches of trees. You had to wade in and get a bit wet, but you could pick up loads of tackle like that.

I told Dad that what I really wanted was a proper bag for my rod and tackle.

'We'll see,' he said, and I knew I was going to get one then. When he said 'no' that meant you couldn't have what you wanted, but 'we'll see' meant that you could although you'd have to wait a bit.

There were brilliant fishing bags advertised in the *Angling Times*. They'd be made of vinyl on the outside to keep your tackle dry from the rain and they had pockets with zips and even a strap for your shoulder.

One morning early in October when it was still dark, Dad came into my room and woke me up on the top bunk really gently.

'Nicky?' His voice pushed its way through the layers of sleep. I opened my eyes and he was right there and he put something blue on the bed. 'There you go, mate. I'm off to the appeal. I'll see you later.'

I was so excited I couldn't stand it. 'Thanks, Dad!'

I watched him leave the room. His big shoulders filled the doorway, and the light was on in the landing behind him.

When I picked up the present, I saw that it wasn't the fishing bag I thought it was. It was a small piece of blue cloth that unrolled itself as I picked it up. It was one of the really cheap fishing rod bags made of light, blue cotton. It was so narrow you couldn't even get your hand inside and it had no pockets, not even a zip. You had to slip your rod in at the top and tie two laces to keep it in. I felt my stomach turn over, not because I was disappointed, but because I felt so sad. He'd got me a fishing bag but he'd got the wrong one.

I really loved him in that moment. I loved my dad because he had tried to get me what I wanted and he'd even woken me up to give it to me before he left, but I felt sad at the same time because it was a crap bag and now he was going again and I couldn't even say thanks properly.

I lay in bed for ages, pressing the blue cloth to my face.

Glan Gerrionedd

The Reluctant Shop Steward

There's a bump in the night. I feel it reverberate through the bare floorboards in my bedroom. My eyes open and I'm disoriented for a moment. Then I remember where I am. Lifting my head from the pillow, I listen and hear him groaning from the other room.

I know what's happened; he's fallen out of bed. Now it's just a question of whether he will make his own way back or if he'll call me for help.

'Nicky!'

Throwing the switch in my bedroom, I steady my sleepy bones as my eyes adjust to the brightness. He's still calling my name when I find my glasses, pull them on and go through to his room.

He's on the floor next to the bed, lifting his head off the bare floorboards. I can see the tension in his neck. His whole body is rigid in spasm and his lips are quivering, his tongue licking as he tries to moisten his mouth and get some breath in his lungs to speak.

'Me pills ...' He gestures with his eyes up to the top of the nightstand by the side of the bed behind him.

I know where he means but something in me prolongs the moment. 'Your pills? Do you want me to get them for you?'

'Me pills!'

'You said that already. Do you want me to get them for you?'

'Nicky!'

My heart is racing and I hate this moment. It irritates me. I want him to get up, not lie there like an invalid. If I push him some part of me thinks he'll find some strength inside and leap out of himself, even though, logically, I know he can't.

Standing over him, I lift him under the armpits. He groans in pain but there's no other way I can think of doing it. I want to slap him for being so pathetic, for disappearing so utterly behind his illness. I get him into a sitting position and now both his hands are shaking violently.

'Pills!'

'In a minute. Let's get you back into bed first.'

'PILLS!'

I move behind him and visualise the path of his backside from the floor onto the mattress and then I make it happen. He's heavy and stiff like warm clay. As soon as he hits the mattress he falls backwards into a foetal curve on the bed. I reach for his small silver pill box and open it. There are blue and yellow and white pills in there.

'Which ones?'

His hands darts out and I put the pill box closer to him so he can see inside. He knocks it out of my hand. The pills scatter all over the bed. His face goes red with anger and he mumbles something obscene.

'What's that?'

He tries again.

'I can't hear you, mate. I'll call out the colours and you groan when I say the right one. Blue?'

'Urgnh!'

Picking a blue pill off his pyjama top, I reach for the glass of water with the straw already in it. Jamming the blue pill between his leathery lips, I push it past his teeth and into his mouth. I lift his head with one hand, and insert the straw between his lips.

He sucks. The water rises in the straw and then falls away before it reaches his mouth. He groans at the failed effort. He sucks again in two, three stages until the water rises up the straw and disappears into his mouth. He doesn't stop sucking until the glass is almost empty. I feel him relax. Letting his head fall back onto the pillow, I want to stroke the sweaty hair off his forehead but can't bring myself to do it. Instead I start picking up the fallen pills from his pyjamas and from within the bedding.

His legs are both shaking in a half-crouch position across the mattress and I reach out and force them straight. They spring back into a crouch. I push them straight again and hold them in place. He is looking with fierce blue eyes and I don't like what I read there.

'What? Am I doing something wrong?'

'Rough bastard.'

'Oh, that's charming, that is. You throw yourself out of bed, get me up in the middle of the night, lob your pills all over the room and then get a cob on because I'm not Florence enough for you!'

He gurgles with amusement. 'Honey sandwich.'

'I'll call room service. Where's the phone?'

'Nicky!'

'All right, I'll be back in a minute.'

Picking up the glass, I head downstairs to the back kitchen, throwing light switches all the way to scatter the midges and moths. I choose the soft sliced bread and put plenty of butter on to help him suck and swallow it. I run the knife through the honey jar and lay on a thick slab of sweetness.

I close the sandwich, slice it in quarters the way he likes and put it on a plate. Then I rinse the glass and fill it with water from the jerry can.

In his first few months in prison Dad kept waiting for guidance from the Communist Party and the union leadership, but it never came. His visitors just told him to keep his head down and leave the campaign to his comrades on the outside.

At Stafford prison, Dad started to take on some of the complaints from fellow inmates about living conditions, harassment from some

171

prison officers and examples of everyday hassles. He became a sort of shop steward for the cons and they would come to him regularly with issues and grievances that they were too afraid to raise themselves.

The first time he went to present a list of complaints to the visiting magistrate, he had made the appointment beforehand as was the custom and had been told that if his complaints and allegations were proved false he would be charged under Rule 47(12), which meant that he would lose remission – effectively adding to his prison term. The pressure built up over the week before his hearing and he had to sign a declaration stating that he understood the consequences of a false allegation. He was invited to withdraw his allegations right up to the last moment before it was 'too late'.

On the day itself he stood in the governor's office flanked by two big security officers who turned their heads so they were breathing on him the whole time. He was nervous. He tried to keep his voice steady and to keep his notes from quivering in his hands. He took issue with instances of squalid, overcrowded living conditions and the misappropriation of food intended for prisoners. He also asked about the profits being made from the purchase of small items by prisoners at the canteen.

He was asked to leave the room. When he returned, the magistrate informed him that the profits were used to buy 'recreational facilities' for the prisoners. Dad smiled at this and glanced at his notes. In his stride now, he stated that in the past two years the only recreational facilities provided had been two dartboards to the combined value of £10, which left a – conservatively estimated – profit of £4,000 over the same period.

There was a cough from the prison governor and an embarrassed silence from the magistrates. Dad pressed his advantage suggesting that it might be a good idea to display a full audit of the canteen takings and profits along with a six-monthly balance sheet on the prison noticeboard to show where the rest of the money had gone and where funds were being spent in future.

The magistrate said he would look into it and set a date when they would meet again. The results of a hearing can only be properly concluded in the presence of the prisoner who has brought the complaint.

Two days later Dad was transferred to another prison. He never saw the magistrate again and no charges of false allegations were brought against him.

I think about this as I walk back into the dimly lit room and see Dad curled up again on the bed moaning softly, although his mouth is clamped shut.

Feeling a stab of unwanted shame and sadness prickling my eyes, I move away from the sensation by striding across the room to sit on the edge of the bed and feed my father one quarter of a honey sandwich, eating the rest myself when he's had enough.

'Was it worth it, Dad? Would you do it again?'

He manoeuvres his lips, pushes out a crust of the sandwich and lets it fall onto his neck. I pick it off and put it on the plate. He pushes saliva onto his lips and makes them work for a moment before he speaks.

'Not now.'

'Not now – you mean you wouldn't do it again now, or you're not going to tell me now?'

He takes a deep breath and straightens his legs over the bed. Pulling the blankets from under him, I lay them over his body up to his neck. He watches me do this.

'Pillow.'

I pick up a pillow from the floor, put on a crazed expression and lower the pillow towards his face. He barks out a laugh. Lifting his head, I place the pillow behind him.

His hand emerges from underneath the blankets and he offers it to me. I take it. He grips my hand in his.

'Good on ye ...'

'You too. See you in the morning.'

I switch the light off on my way out and go downstairs to turn all the other lights off.

I climb into my own bed and lie with my hands behind my head. There's a big moth banging itself against the lampshade of my bedside light but I haven't got the heart to kill it.

The next morning it is cold and the fire hasn't yet warmed up the room so Dad's wearing a blanket and cradling a cup of tea in his hands.

In the run-up to Christmas 1974 Dad and Ricky were sick of reading resolutions to the Home Secretary and they had a meeting in their cell in Sudbury. They decided the union leadership needed a push. They agreed to refuse to wear prison clothes or to do prison labour and to apply for status as political prisoners. There was nothing else they could do on the inside.

On the morning of Christmas Eve they were taken to isolation cells, where they stripped off their prison uniforms and donned blankets before they were visited by the governor.

'I told him the TUC had demanded our release by Christmas,' he recalls, 'and it didn't look like that was about to happen so we assumed the movement would be stepping up the campaign and me and Ricky were acting in solidarity.'

They were banged up in isolation for twenty-four hours a day with no exercise for three days before being called before the governor. The first thing he asked my dad was his number.

'I gave him my social security number. The chairman of the magistrates checked his records and asked for my prison number. I told him that's not my number that's your number. He asks me how I plead

174

to the charge of not wearing prison clothes. I say not guilty. He looks at me in my blanket and asks me how I can plead not guilty! I tell him that charge is from prison rules for convicted criminals. I am a political prisoner so those rules don't apply to me. The same goes for the charge of refusing prison labour.'

'What happened?'

'Guilty on both counts. Another thirty-five days in jail and back down to the isolation cell. Then they moved me to Lincoln and let me wear my own clothes but kept me in solitary. Five months with no family visits, just MPs and the newspapers to let me know what was going on outside. Then I got the letter from Ricky.'

Prison rules made it impossible for one prisoner to write to another prisoner but this letter was hand-delivered by a prison officer. Ricky's letter said that he had decided to come off the protest and to wear prison clothes, do prison labour and go for parole to continue the fight from the outside. He urged Dad to do the same.

Dad never knew about the pressure from the friends and political advisers that Ricky was put under to give up the protest and write that letter in the hope of convincing Dad to do the same.

Dad thought about it. He spent hours, then days staring at the dark brick walls, pacing out the four or five steps of his cell, listening for the occasional clink of keys and the clack of boots on the concrete floor as his meals were brought in and his pot was taken to be emptied. The bricks, the light bulb, the thoughts of outside, home, the fight and the silence. Pacing up and down. Thinking it over. Being tempted.

'I weighed it up and thought about the message that would be sent out if I gave in. And that was it,' he says.

He asked to see his solicitor and made a statement saying that he believed to give in now would make a mockery of the protest and would be betrayal of all the people who were struggling hard for his unconditional release as a political prisoner.

'I couldn't have done time with a better man. It was the only time we ever disagreed on any action in all the time we were inside.'

The bricks, the light bulb, the footsteps, the keys, the food, the slops, the pacing up and down, the cold winter wind on a cool grey skin. And then another letter, this time from Bert Ramelson of the Communist Party, asking him to cease the protest and thus remove the Home Secretary's excuse for not giving in to their demands for his release.

A sick feeling of apprehension. A weary sleeplessness through the nights that followed until he picked up a copy of the *Morning Star*. There he read Ramelson's letter to him, now presented as his own words, explaining why he had decided to call off the protest along with Ricky.

Outmanoeuvred, outplayed and out of step with the wishes of his own party, he sent a message to the governor saying he would wear the clothes and do the labour. But he wasn't going to press for parole.

'The next day my prison greys arrived and I climbed into them. I waited to be taken to a normal cell with normal privileges – but that didn't happen. All they did was give me half an hour's exercise a day. On my own in the yard surrounded by screws and their dogs.'

Bus stop

The morning after Dad was put away again I was strolling down our road to the village shop to get breakfast.

The day was full of low-hanging cloud, cold and wet on the face. The whole world was grey and damp. I looked up the silent driveway to where the vicarage stood somewhere beyond the mist. I passed the little house where the miserable Mr and Mrs Ord lived, a retired couple who wanted 'nothing to do with communists or their children'. On past the deserted house in the middle of our street next to the vacant lot behind the E.C. Evans tractor shop full of abandoned parts twisted and rusting in the weather. On to the corner near the petrol pumps and the old church. There just around the corner was a bus stop with a bunch of kids in school uniforms and a couple of grown-ups waiting for the bus to take them to Denbigh.

They all stopped talking and looked at me in silence. I slowed down but there was no turning back so I walked on and muttered a greeting to some of the kids I recognised from school. They looked away.

They were all dead embarrassed. I was embarrassed as well. I wanted to feel proud but I couldn't. In London or Liverpool or even Chester I could feel proud because there people knew what was going on. They knew my dad was a hero. But in Henllan I felt embarrassed because they just thought my dad was in prison.

Wanker

Shortly after Dad had gone back inside a man called John Llywarch, one of the Shrewsbury pickets, came to take us to his farmhouse for a few days.

We drove there with us five kids all bunched up in the back of his van, Mum in the front. The car had bad petrol fumes and the roads were rutted and bumpy for a lot of the way through the Welsh mountains on the way to his farm.

Starting to feel sick and wanting to vomit, I told them this a few times but it didn't make any difference.

'We're nearly there.'

A cold sweat on my face and my head started to ache. For some terrible reason I leaned over and aimed into Andy's lap. He had to sit in it until we arrived and I tried not to scream with perverse laughter.

The man had a big farmhouse with outbuildings and a wife and two kids a bit younger than me and Andy. A big fire in the sitting room with chipboard cuttings. It was a warm house and he and his wife were very nice.

One night me and Andy had to go and have a bath and he ran it for us and then waited for us to get undressed and get in the bath. We were a bit nervous because we'd never got undressed in front of a stranger before and I kept saying that we weren't ready yet.

He was laughing and being all friendly and told us there was nothing to worry about and we didn't need to be shy. Then he asked us if either of us had started wanking yet. I mumbled that I didn't know what wanking was and he said that was ridiculous.

'You're thirteen and you haven't had a pull? Come on, I'll show you.'

He locked the bathroom door and unzipped himself over the toilet bowl. He was already aroused and he said we could touch it if we wanted. We didn't. He told us not to worry, it would be all right, but we just stared as he started playing with himself.

When he'd finished he wiped himself off and flushed the toilet.

'Have a go by yourselves tonight.'

Then he left the bathroom and I locked the door behind him. Andy said he didn't like him and I said we had to be careful because he was one of Dad's mates and he was probably all right.

On the road

We went to a lot of meetings and rallies and marches all over the country as part of the campaign to get Dad and Ricky released. We visited union offices to meet with union leaders who would give us fairy cakes and tell us that they were doing everything in their power.

We'd all sit there and I'd try to smile and believe them. We swallowed everything with strong tea.

We visited the Houses of Parliament to have meetings with MPs. They'd take us to the restaurant in parliament to drink tea and eat sandwiches off special green crockery with pictures of a little prison gate on.

We went to universities and polytechnics to meet student union leaders with accents that were so thick I could only understand what they were saying because I had heard the same things from so many other people.

'It's a watershed conviction.'

'We've got to mobilise the masses.'

'It won't end here.'

'We're calling for a General Strike.'

'The miners'll be next.'

I collected loads of badges: Free Angela Davis; Fight the National Front; Free the Shrewsbury Pickets (which became Free the Shrewsbury Three, then Free the Shrewsbury Two, then finally Free Des Warren).

One time I was at the head of a march of 13,000 workers through the streets of London. This was the end of a famously long and tortuous march from Wigan to London, organised by the WRP but attended and supported by workers from across the spectrum. I was lifted up and put onto the shoulders of a man at the front. Behind me I could see a human snake twisted down the road with police barriers on either side. I could feel the power of so many voices shouting for my dad's release. It filled my head and my heart with a thrill I had never imagined before and I wished all the people back in Henllan could see this on the news.

Then the police opened the barricade at the end of Downing Street to let us and our mum through. I could hear all the voices behind filling London. I watched Mum walk up the steps to hand the envelope to someone at Number 10. They took it quickly and closed the door. I was amazed that nothing happened. I thought my dad was going to walk out right then and there. It was obvious everybody wanted him out of prison.

Striking the pose

Everybody told me that my dad was a hero of the working class and I knew they were right but I didn't know what to do about it.

Until one day when I was sitting in the front row of another boring conference in London. I had my pretend leather jacket over one of my dad's old turtleneck sweaters that was now full of badges, and was watching a union leader explain to an angry crowd why they couldn't reverse the scales of justice.

My heart was beating fast and I wanted to stand up and shout at him. Instead I felt my hand curl up into a fist with the thumb under my chin. It was a pose that my dad used when he was listening or thinking.

Out of the corner of my eye, I saw a photographer walking up to me from my left. I held the pose and pretended I couldn't see him. I didn't want to break the spell of being my dad. The camera flashed and in that moment I knew what I had to do.

I had to be my dad. I had to listen and nod and pretend I knew what was going on. I had to know who was good and who was bad and what was right and what was wrong. I had to know who was to blame, and that was the easiest part. The people to blame were all the people who weren't talking to you.

With that photograph I vanished into the folds of the oversized, hand-me-down turtleneck sweater where I could hide for as long as I needed to.

Every time we visited Dad in prison he'd look at me for a moment and ask me about how school was going. 'Get yourself an education, mate,' he'd say.

So I did. I enjoyed those years at Denbigh High School. I made some friends, did my bit on the sports field, answered questions about my dad, worried about looking good, bragged about girls and argued about music. It kept me busy, and for weeks, sometimes even months at a time I learned not to think about my dad at all until something else happened and we all had to react.

The head of serenity

Mum was on tranquillisers and sleeping pills now and her hair was falling out. She spent most of her time in her room lying in bed. She'd run the house by shouting out instructions or calling one of us for an audience – usually me. In her bedroom she had a collection of wigs that looked like the same head of hair made into different styles.

The one she used most of the time was a blonde, frizzy thing, and she wore it when we went to visit Dad, to meetings and on marches. When she wasn't wearing it she kept it on a polystyrene head on the dressing table of her bedroom. The head was white with eyes, a nose and mouth but no ears; it looked like somebody very calm and nearly asleep.

I would sneak in there to look at it sometimes when Mum was out of the house or in the bath. I'd smell the wig and pull out the pins that kept it in place. The tiny slick sound as the pins came out of the frizzy folds of fake hair was somehow satisfying.

Once, when the house was quiet and everybody was out

except Bruce the dog, I put the wig on. I stepped out onto the landing and walked down the stairs. Through the banister I could see Bruce lying on the floor of the dining room under the table and when I got to the bottom I called his name.

He saw me and started to growl. A ridge of hair stood upright down his back and his lips curled up over his teeth. Then he leaped towards me. Whipping off the wig, I backed away up the stairs and he stopped.

Putting the wig back on the Head of Serenity, I pushed a few pins in to keep it in place. Then, closing the bedroom door behind me, I went back downstairs and took the dog brush from the cupboard and ran it through Bruce's fur out in the back yard. Great swathes of blonde hairs swam in the breeze and up my nose.

Paul Smith

As the oldest it was my job to take Bruce for a walk every day: once in the morning before school, once in the evening when I got home and a big walk on Saturday and Sunday.

Bruce and I had our own things going on in our heads and so mostly we'd lope around the village in silence, but sometimes when I took the route over the field into the woods we'd sit down for a while and have a bit of a chat. It was on one of these thirty-minute walks that I first met Paul Smith.

He had just moved into the area and lived in one of the new houses in the development on the far edge of the village. He was tall and blond with long legs and he was also walking a dog, a beagle called Whisky. Paul was the same age as me but he was going to school in Abergele. We acknowledged each other as we met, then fell into step and struck up an easy conversation.

His mum was Scottish and his dad English, a retired sergeant major from the army. (He was a big man with an easy smile but a short temper, and he was a stickler for discipline.) Paul also had an older sister with big bones who was going into the police.

I'd never smoked because my dad said it was 'a mug's game', but I remember standing on the top of the slope looking down over the field to the edge of Garn Woods where the big house was and Paul pulled out his packet of Benson & Hedges and offered me one and lit it for me.

Taking the smoke into my mouth, I let it stay there for a while before I let it drift out of my nostrils. It tasted fantastic. Instantly I became light-headed and began to feel a rush of blood and the increasing pressure of an erection. Suddenly all those movie scenes where two people lit up after sex made sense to me and I was hooked, not just on the rebellion of the act, but on that astounding chemical reaction, which never happened again.

Paul became a great friend except when we'd compete for the same girl or fall into arguments about who had the best dog.

Often we'd let our dogs go off the leads to see which was the fastest runner until they started to bother the cows and then we'd see who could call the loudest and whose dog was the most obedient. We'd stand and shout, 'Bruce!' and

'Whisky!' like two alcoholics trying to get the attention of a deaf barman.

Paul had the widest flares I'd ever seen until one day he turned up in the tightest pair of drainpipes on earth and I laughed for about a week.

Then I took the scissors and the sewing kit to transform my own trousers into the new style.

School uniform

I liked uniforms. I liked the way you could disappear inside a uniform and have only your own thoughts running around your head. I liked the way uniforms made you look smart, and most of all the way they made you feel like you were a part of something.

I liked my school uniform. And when I grew too big for it I liked going to the stuffy old shop in town to get my new one.

I liked the way the tailor measured me up and selected the trousers, and the feel of the carpet under my bare feet as I walked around to check I had the right length. The way he slipped the blazer over my shoulders and told me to move my arms. The way he tugged on the sleeves and told me there was growing room. I liked the smell of the new material and I liked the brown paper bag into which he folded it all with a gentle pat.

The only thing I didn't like was the look on his face when I handed over the chit from the Department of Health and Social Security to pay for it all.

Ricky

Ricky got out of prison in July 1975, just before my fourteenth birthday, and he came to see Mum with some of his mates.

Seeing Ricky in our front room was exciting because he was so big. He was also loud and he laughed a lot and he talked fast and he had loads to say and he wasn't going to stop till our dad was out as well.

He told us loads of funny things about being in jail and how Dad was such a snarler and always giving the screws a hard time – just like they did to Mr Mackay from *Porridge*. They all hated him for putting them on charges all the time. It sounded all right really.

At the end he got serious. He gave Mum a big hug and called her 'She' and 'Queen', and then he shook my hand. 'Don't worry, Nicky lad,' he said. 'We'll get him out in no time.'

We were all dead excited when he left because Ricky was like a magnet and loads of lads hung around him and they all had plans. Then we'd read about him and see pictures of him in the papers and he was always up and shouting and pointing and calling for action. Once we saw him on telly being dragged out of the TUC Conference for causing a disturbance and he was telling everyone they ought to be ashamed.

I thought he was great for doing that. He was embarrassing everyone for keeping my dad inside. Then the camera moved away from him to the stony faces in the audience and the people on the stage who were coughing and trying to ignore him. I knew then that even Ricky couldn't do anything.

Mum wrote a letter to Dad and asked him to stop fighting everyone in prison. She asked him to think about his family, to say he was sorry and to come home. She told me all the things she'd said in the letter and I was glad I hadn't written it. I knew it was wrong.

Mum knew it was wrong as well and the next day she was on the phone to the governor. She told him to tear up the letter and not to give it to Dad.

Acting the goat

In the summer after school you could go to the bus stop and get the bus home, or you could hang around with your friends and smoke cigarettes and talk about stuff.

The first time I accepted the invitation to hang around with Neil Chinnery and Johnny Fish I got home after seven o'clock and I thought Mum would go mad. But she just called me into her bedroom where all the kids were sitting round eating cheese and biscuits off paper plates so there would be no washing-up.

'Where have you been?'

'Up by the castle with friends.'

'That sounds nice.'

I looked at Andy in amazement.

The next day Andy stayed out after school and didn't come back till later, but Mum shouted at him and sent him to our room for the rest of the night with no telly.

That's when I realised there were some major benefits to being the oldest. Until that moment it hadn't occurred to me to do anything because I'd always get shouted at and punished by Mum or Uncle Bob. Or even worse I'd get that disappointed look from Dad on a prison visit.

'Don't go acting the goat,' he'd say.

But I hadn't seen my dad for months now. He was in solitary. Somewhere in the back of my mind I thought that if I was careful I could get away with anything. All I had to do was try it and see what happened.

I was taller than Mum already and she was always tired or depressed or distracted or sleeping. So long as I made the odd cup of tea, did the washing-up and dealt with the kids every now and then I was pretty much a free agent.

I grew apart from my brothers and sisters from then on. I started to see them as kids who were just getting in the way of what could be my very own life.

New cadet

One evening after school, I was with Neil Chinnery and Johnny Fish up by Denbigh Castle near the mental home, smoking Consulate cigarettes and watching Johnny's girlfriend having a pee behind a parked car.

Neil came up with the idea of joining the Air Training Corps and training to become a pilot in the RAF. Johnny wasn't so keen because his glasses had really thick lenses and he was nearly blind, but I only wore my glasses to see the blackboard and read books so I said I was up for it.

Neil and me joined up. We had to meet the warrant officer and his second-in-command, then we had to stand up and salute the Union Jack and pledge allegiance to the Crown.

I was really glad I'd left my turtleneck sweater with all the badges on at home, and all the time I tried not to think about Dad, who, on his first day at trial, had refused to stand for the Queen to hear the charges against him. He'd told them he'd stand for the Queen if they stood for the trade union movement – and they did.

Instead I tried to think about the uniform and going on parade near the bus stop where girls could see you, learning how to march and fire a rifle, and how the whole thing would be like an adventure and even better than Boy Scouts. It wasn't like I was going in the army where I could be ordered to break strikes by emptying the bins or running the fire engines. It was just a laugh.

But then we had an eyesight test and I had to put my glasses on. The warrant officer rested his baton on my shoulder and looked at me carefully. I thought he could see all the things I was thinking and that he was going to tell me they don't accept communists in the Air Force, but he said something even worse instead: 'Know this, Warren: you'll never be a pilot, but you can still go a long way as ground crew in the Air Force. Carry on.'

So I learned how to march. I learned how to fire a .22 rifle at a target. ('Five rounds in your own time – carry on!') I learned about wind speeds and cloud formations with great names like nimbostratus, and how to shout out answers to simple questions. ('Speak up that man!') Then one day I got to go in the bus all the way out past Chester, past Ellesmere Port to the Wirral, where I was loaded into the back seat of a Jet Provost and taken up. It was brilliant.

The helmet was leather with earphones built in and it made our voices scratchy and heroic and somehow urgent and clipped. We went higher than the broken clouds and looked right down on the complex sprawl of industrial England. All the while the pilot was talking to me, explaining things and I didn't hear a word he was saying until he barked at me to take the controls.

I had control of my own plane for nearly a minute before we started banking quite steeply and he told me to pull her up. I did, but too fast and we nearly flipped over. He told me to do everything slowly and gently, so we started heading down towards a steaming factory tower until he lost his nerve and wrestled the controls off me.

On the way back in the bus we were all chatting up a storm about what had happened and how we'd done. It felt great to be sitting there wearing the same uniform and sharing an experience with lads from all over North Wales.

Then word got round to the big lads in the back seats who my dad was. I was 'invited' up to join the crowd from Wrexham at the back of the bus.

Somebody moved out of a seat and let me take his place. It was all quiet and they were all staring at me with the cold eyes that boys put on when they're acting hard. I had to turn right round in my seat and kneel to face the lad on the back seat who was talking to me.

'Is it true your dad's a commie?'

It all crashed in that moment. Suddenly it felt like I was in enemy territory and it wasn't a game. I could pretend my dad wasn't a communist or maybe say that he was but that I wasn't.

'Yeah, he is. Yeah,' I said.

'All commies are bastards.'

It was like the first slap in the face, a warm-up for what could follow. I thought of loads of ways I could try and get out of this but I didn't use any of them. 'No. That's like saying all Welshmen are sheep-shaggers.' I said.

There was some snuffling and laughing from the back row but not from the big lad who kept his eyes on me. I thought if there was going to be a fight it would be quick because the officers on the bus would stop it almost at once, but then again, I couldn't be sure.

But instead of smacking me in the face he smiled at me like a friend. It was worse. 'Do you want to play knuckles?'

All the lads on the back seat said, 'Ooooooh.' Others started to gather round to watch. I saw that most of them had homemade tattoos and hairy arms. Even the zits on their faces and necks looked aggressive and poisonous.

I said I didn't know what 'knuckles' was. He said the rules were simple. He turned his hand into a fist and told me to do the same. Then we butted our fists up against each other: 'You have to try and smash my knuckles with your fist. If I move away and you miss, it's my go. If I miss then it's your go.'

'What if you don't miss?'

'You keep going until you miss.'

Neil came up behind me and told me quietly to come back to my seat and leave it alone, but I ignored him. I looked into the eyes of this big lad and I hated him. I imagined him in a prison officer's uniform and that made it easier to stay.

We squared up fists and I tried to smash his knuckles. But I missed. Then it was his turn. It never stopped being his turn. He smashed me all over the top of my hands again and again, and after the first few times the shock and the pain went away and I started to like it.

I liked the way he got more and more worked up about it. I liked the way all the other lads started saying, 'That's enough now' and 'Leave the lad alone, for Christ's sake.' I liked the way I just stared at him and at the other lads and even looked off out of the window like I couldn't be bothered. I was saying, 'You can't hurt me.' And he knew it.

Then some of the skin started to come off the back of my hand all around the blue-black bruise that was spreading wider and wider. He went to go in for another smash but held his fist in the air. We looked at each other and he broke the silence: 'You're all right, mate.'

I moved back to my seat and watched the sun go down behind the black trees, roofs, cars and streets, and the brown clouds breaking up against a blackening sky.

I left the Corps a few days after that but I kept the uniform for years. I never told Dad about any of it.

Grandad

Throughout Dad's trial and his time in prison, Grandad was in two minds. He'd lived in Chester all his life, apart from when he went to the Falkland Islands during the Second World War and a few holidays in Spain. He worked on the railways and was a proud man. Proud of his country, of his wife, his life, his kids and his grandchildren. He and Dad used to argue a lot, and Dad always managed to make him lose his temper.

We'd sit in the lounge at Nan and Grandad's flat and Dad would talk about the capitalist laws under which he would be tried. He said they were the first volley in a general attack on the union movement and Grandad would get hot and bothered and bang the arm of his chair: 'We've got the finest legal system in the world!'

So it was very difficult for Grandad when his only son was sent to prison for picketing.

Grandad taught me how to iron my own shirts. He taught me that – when the time came – it was best to stand at the bar so you could feel how much you'd been drinking. He taught me that you only spoil a Scotch by adding ice like the Americans. He taught me how to roast a chicken.

When he came with us on one of the biggest marches to the Houses of Parliament he taught me how one man can hold two opposite beliefs and suffer, but still survive.

Glan Gerrionedd

Prison Issues

He's asleep with his mouth open. He flinches every now and then, from his dreams or his Parkinson's, I don't know. I look at his feet swathed in thick socks inserted into specially severed slippers to give him plenty of room. The fire burns quietly in the grate with the occasional shuffle of logs falling into place as they are consumed. The room smells of smoke and wood sap and listening hard I can hear the natural nothingness of the land around us.

He spent the last six months of his sentence in solitary confinement. In all he was charged thirty-six times by prison officers for petty misdemeanours and had been moved fifteen times to ten different prisons.

In Nottingham prison the convicts were allowed to wear any shoes they liked. This was good news for Dad as he couldn't wear prison issue shoes on medical grounds on account of his high arches. Dad wore slippers or trainers most of the time. He was walking along a landing when a screw noticed his footwear and asked him why he wasn't wearing prison issue slip-ons. Dad explained that he couldn't wear the slip-ons and had lost his prison issue lace-up shoes in the move to Nottingham. The screw snarled.

'I'll see you in prison issue shoes if it's the last thing I do, Warren.'

The next day he was working on his plastering course when he was ordered to follow the screw to collect a pair of prison issue slip-ons. Dad refused and was placed on a charge for refusing an order and lost two weeks' remission.

At the hearing that followed, despite the medical information about his high instep he was ordered to wear prison issue slip-ons whenever required by a prison officer.

He was led out of the hearing by a prison officer who put on a big smile.

'Oh by the way, there'll be no telly for you tonight either, you're going back to solitary, you bad lad!'

Back in his cell he thought about his treatment since he'd arrived at Nottingham and how it had become worse since the mass demonstration to parliament. He decided to go on a two-week hunger strike in protest at the victimisation.

It is not an offence to go on hunger strike and it is normal practice for a prisoner on hunger strike to be taken off work duty and to be left isolated in his cell.

Instead the next morning a prison officer came to collect him to return to work on his plastering course. Dad thought about it for a moment and realised that the screw was waiting for him to refuse labour which is an offence. He got up and went to work.

After four days working without food he was feeling weak when the same screw approached him and told him he had been given a different job. Dad thought they were probably going to give him lighter work because he wasn't eating but in fact the opposite was true.

They made him hang steel cell doors on the third storey of a cell block. He could hardly walk up the stairs without feeling dizzy and bilious with exhaustion and the screws stood around watching him take the stairs carrying the huge steel doors.

'Get up them stairs, you lazy bastard!'

After eight days with no food doing this heavy work Dad could hardly walk without having to stop and balance himself and fight the effects of growing malnutrition. An officer came to tell him that his family were here for a visit and he was led back to his cell to change. He stumbled past screws who were munching on sandwiches.

'Come on, you lazy bastard, get a move on.'

As he stepped outside his cell in his trainers the screw smiled and raised his hand.

'Get your prison shoes on or you're going nowhere.'

Dad explained once again why he couldn't wear the prison shoes and the screw widened his eyes and spoke slowly as if to a child.

'How many times do you have to be told? If you don't wear the shoes you don't get the visit. Do you want me to say it in Russian?'

Dad looked at him for a moment and then made his decision. He stepped into his cell where he got changed back into his work clothes, pushed past the screw in the doorway and went back to work.

The Sheriff of Nottingham

We hadn't been able to visit Dad for five months because he had been in solitary due to his refusal to wear prison clothes or do prison labour. Even after he put the uniform on they wouldn't let him out of solitary so he said he wanted to do a plastering course and they moved him to Nottingham prison where we were allowed to visit.

We had been travelling on buses and trains since about seven in the morning by the time we finally all got into the waiting room. Andy and me were dead keen to see Nottingham and were telling each other stories about Robin Hood and the Sheriff. We'd already decided that we were going to make bows and arrows when we got home. We were excited because we hadn't seen Dad for ages.

All the other visitors went in to see their dads and we were still waiting when they all came out again an hour later. By this time Christy and Kate were getting difficult and Mum kept pestering the prison officer to find out what the problem was. He said our visit had been cancelled because Dad had refused to wear proper prison shoes. He said maybe she should send him a note telling him to wear the shoes.

'Give me a pen and paper and I'll tell him that under no circumstances should he put up with any intimidation,' she replied. 'He's never worn prison shoes on any of our visits to this day.'

Dad couldn't wear prison shoes because of the shape of his feet. He even had a prison medical certificate to prove it. We waited another hour before Mum decided she'd had enough. We were about to leave when the officer said we could go in and have our visit now.

Dad looked like a scarecrow. I couldn't stop staring at his wrists where the skin was stretched over the bones. The visiting room was empty except for the prison officers standing around watching us, listening to Dad explain about the hunger strike he was on, the shoes he refused to wear and the heavy work he was having to do. He'd been on hunger strike before, but he'd never looked this bad.

'I've been off the food for eight days,' he told us, 'but they won't take me off work duty like they normally do. They've got me hanging cell doors up on Level Three. I'm up and down stairs all day carrying these steel doors and I'm not up to it, to be honest.'

'Why don't you refuse?'

'That's what they want. If I refuse prison labour they'll charge me and I'm not gonna give them the satisfaction.'

Mum was trying not to cry in front of us. She lifted her head high instead and took both of Dad's hands in hers. 'Eight days hard labour with no food! Dennis, they're trying to kill you.'

I wished she'd just cried instead of saying that because that made me really scared.

When the visit was over Mum demanded to see the governor. He refused so she said they were going to stay there until he agreed to see her. 'And so you had better get food for my children because we're not leaving.'

By this time all the fun of being in Robin Hood's city was gone and we all started getting bored and scared.

Labour MP Tom Litterick and his wife Jane arrived then, and you could see the prison officers standing straighter and looking a bit nervous as Mum told Tom what was going on.

Then the prison officer said that the governor had sent a message that Tom couldn't see Mum on prison premises so they went outside and left us with Jane. We didn't know Jane but we did know that we were in prison and our mum was outside.

When Mum and Tom tried to come back inside the prison they weren't allowed in on the governor's orders. A prison officer went outside to explain this to Mum and as he was talking she ducked past him and ran into the prison. Later we all thought it was dead funny that she must be the only woman ever to sneak into a prison when most people wanted to sneak out.

Mum asked for food again and some blankets because we were going to stay there all night until the governor agreed to meet her. Instead they let Tom back in and between them they agreed to let Tom see Dad and he would tell all the MPs in the House of Commons so we could leave.

By the time we got out it was nearly dark and it was too late to go and see the castle where the Sheriff of Nottingham had all his adventures with Robin Hood but Mum said it didn't matter.

We heard later that the governor had Dad taken down to the punishment cell after our visit and started the paperwork to have him moved to the punishment block at Lincoln prison.

Book-worming

I started reading all the time. The books I chose from the library had to have a good cover and title, and they had to be small enough to fit into my blazer pocket.

I had a book with me all the time and it meant I could sit on the school bus and keep my head down and not have to talk to anyone. I could go into somebody else's story and forget about what was going on in my life.

I would read at the bus stop before the bus arrived. I'd read on the toilet. I'd read in assembly before the sermon started. I'd read over lunchtime. I'd read while I was babysitting my brothers and sisters.

Sometimes I'd get so into a book that I'd start to think about it when I wasn't even reading it. I'd start to think like the main character and I'd have that character in my head so they could look at my world and help me come up with great ways to deal with it. I didn't feel like the main character in my own life. I didn't feel like a hero. I felt like I was only pretending and that deep down I was a total coward.

One of the books I read was called *My Side of the Mountain* about a boy who ran away from home and went to live in the Catskill mountains on his own. He had to make things he needed like tools and clothes, and learn how to hunt for fish and meat, grow vegetables and scavenge for fruit and berries. He had a lot of thoughts going on in his head but he didn't have any time to deal with them because he had to think about eating, staying warm, keeping away from strangers and watching out for wild animals.

Badly wanting to do the same, I looked at maps of the area around Henllan to see how big the woods were and imagine how long I could stay in there without being found.

I used to walk further into the woods with Bruce, but every time I found a stretch that looked deserted I'd come across tyre tracks or a pheasant coop or a fuel dump or used shotgun cartridges or a farmhouse or a fence overlooking a busy road and I'd give up and go home.

Glan Gerrionedd

Amnesty and Medication

On 14 July 1975 Dad's solicitor received a letter from Amnesty International. They had decided to adopt him as a political prisoner. The letter from Angela Wright, Western European Research Department, read:

> We have decided to 'adopt' Dennis Warren. As you probably know, it is a rule of Amnesty International that members of the organisation do not work for causes in their own country. We are giving the case to a European Amnesty group who will appeal to the British Government for Dennis Warren's release, help support the family and publicise the case in their country.

It was a great day. It was in the papers and everything. At school the lads were amazed at the idea of there being such thing as a political prisoner in Great Britain.

People couldn't believe it, and even the the *Daily Telegraph* looked into it and reported that Dad's case was to be taken up by a group of French lawyers.

Three months later, a group of Labour MPs raised the issue in Parliament. The Home Office undersecretary leaped to her feet to utter a firm denial. Amnesty International had not formally or even provisionally adopted Dennis Warren as a political prisoner and they are sorry for the error in communication.

I wonder if this acceptance and then rejection by Amnesty International added to his later decision to take the medicine that was to affect him for the rest of his life.

I wake late and there's a clattering of pans coming from downstairs. Dad's doing the washing-up. I lie for a while not wanting to get down there till he's finished but I'm thirsty and I need coffee.

When I get into the back kitchen the kettle is still hot. I spark up the stove to bring it back to the boil, then I pick up a dishcloth and start drying the pots and pans.

Dad moves away from the sink and starts tapping the walls with a fist. 'You could do a lot with this place.'

'Yeah?'

'Knock out some decent-sized windows. Take some of the walls out and open it up a bit. Get some hot water plumbed in.'

'Shall we have a go?'

'I'd love to. Get a gang of lads here for a month.'

He stares out of the window for a moment. The yard is a scruffy scattering of splintered kindling and abandoned tools.

'What are you going to do, Dad?'

'Just carry on, mate. See where this Parky takes me.'

He clenches and unclenches his fist speculatively.

At the end of February 1976 Dad arrived at Leicester prison. The Home Secretary had arranged the move in the hope that he could 'establish more satisfactory relations with prison staff'.

When he arrived at the reception area, the admissions officer picked up his prison file, which was now ten inches thick, and said, 'Christ, who have we got here?'

They told him he was to be moved into a cell with another inmate and he refused immediately. Dad hated sharing with other cons because they got on his nerves. He just wanted to be on his own. They told him they didn't have any single cells. He told them to move him to another prison and was asked to wait.

'Eventually this bleeder takes me down to a single cell, unlocks it and steps aside,' he tells me now. 'It's been used for drug addicts and alcoholics. It's a right mess. There's shit everywhere – all over old bits of clothing and newspaper and it stinks. The screw tells me he'll get it cleaned up and he calls over this old fellah working the landing with a bucket. I know what they're playing at. Word gets out that I let an old con clean my cell and I'll be marked by the others so I tell him I'll do it myself. Then they take me to see a doctor.'

He stares at his hand again. We both do.

'I go into his office and he's standing behind his desk. There's these thick curtains drawn across the window and a little desk lamp. It's dark. This doctor asks me how am I. I tell him I've had two years of victimisation from screws in ten different prisons, I've been moved nearly twenty times, spent eight months in solitary confinement, undergone two hunger strikes and now my wife's in hospital being treated for nervous exhaustion and my kids have been taken into care. I tell him I'm beginning to feel the strain and if they bang me up with another con who might well have problems of his own there might be a bit of a scene.'

'What does he say?'

'He writes me a prescription. I tell him I don't want drugs. I've seen the other cons on drugs and I want none of it. I just want a single cell. He tells me he'll keep the prescription on file and I can get it if I need it.'

Dad opens his fists and watches his fingers spread wide. He holds his hands out and stares at them. There's a slight tremor but it's not bad at the moment. 'That's how all this started.'

I don't say anything, but put the pan down quietly. He stuffs his hands into his pockets and carries on.

'I asked for a phone call so I could speak to your mum in hospital. I knew Ricky used to call Marlene all the time when he was in Leicester and the deputy governor said there shouldn't be a problem. Then he sent me a note saying the Home Office had refused to allow the call.

'They put this eastern European immigrant into the cell with me. He couldn't speak English and I didn't think he was the full shilling. I had to make his bed for him and he could never remember how to do it. He used to wash in my dirty water. I said he shouldn't be in prison at all. I felt sorry for the fellah but he was driving me up the wall. The only way I could get a cell on my own was if I went on hunger strike; then they've got to move you to a single cell. So I went on hunger strike and they moved him. I came off hunger strike and they put me back in my cell with an epileptic lad. Epileptics are supposed to be in special cells with special furniture and constant supervision. He had fits all the time and I was forever up and down, pulling his tongue out of his mouth and fucking about at all hours so I went on hunger strike again. Bastards were really piling it on.'

We're driving to a phone box in town at Dad's request. He is getting bored and maybe a little anxious. All these questions about the past are beginning to affect him. He wants to go home early.

I take his elbow and lead him across the road to the telephone box. We move slowly because he can't widen his steps. The frailty and surrender his shuffling implies annoys me. I swing him round a little too briskly and deposit him in the phone box. He lands hard up against the instrument and I hear him chuckle. His laughter is hiding his embarrassment and it helps me find a crack of light in what is a very dark mood that has come between us.

I watch him fumble in his pocket for small change. His tongue is sticking out ever so slightly with the effort of trying to co-ordinate the fingers of his right hand into a pinching position to pick out the coins that I can hear jingling just out of reach in the pockets of his jacket.

I dip my hand into the pocket of my jeans and bring out a selection of coins. I push him aside and slip a few into the slot. 'Do you want me to dial for you as well?'

It comes out a lot harder than I had meant it to, but instead of answering he shoulders me out of the way and hides the instrument from view. 'Close the door, you nosy bastard.'

I step outside and turn my back on the wind to roll a cigarette. I try to hear his conversation, which is impossible.

He's phoning one of his women. I haven't met this one yet, and somehow I can never remember the names of any of the women that I hear about or even the ones I have briefly met on my infrequent visits home. They take me into their arms and smile broadly in that irritating, conspiratorial way that makes me a part of the temporary dalliance that they all feel sure is so permanent.

When I turn my head I can see his lips moving and I wonder how he does it. How does he attract these women into his diminishing life with such regularity and ease?

As I'm standing there now I think back on one of my favourite stories of him driving an old Mark II Jag through the Cheshire countryside on a dark, cloudy night in his early twenties with a girlfriend in the passenger seat. He takes a corner too fast and crashes through a hedge into a ploughed field. They step out of the car and make their way towards the lights of the farmhouse. The farmer makes them tea to calm their nerves and lets Dad use the telephone to call a taxi while he takes his lantern out into the field and inspects the damage to the hedge, which he says will grow back, and to the car, which needs new suspension.

They drink tea, wait for the taxi and listen to the farmer's tales of woe: crop failures; infestations; bad weather; and falling market prices.

When the taxi arrives Dad throws the car keys on the kitchen table. 'You can have it, mate. Sorry for the trouble.'

I always thought it a romantic story, even if I could never bury a deep wish that he'd kept the car and given it to me. I think that right now as I shiver outside the phone box, watching my dad's lips move.

He stands over the basin in the bathroom swilling the hairs out of the bowl with the plastic jug. He's wearing his training pants, which are baggy at the knees with wear (of whoever it was that donated them to the charity shop). I can see little love handles spreading over the sides. His skin is pale, and his broad back and shoulders are hunched as he concentrates on getting every shaved piece of hair down the plughole – it's an old habit, a dirty sink could cost you an extra week in prison.

Towards the end of his sentence, Dad was given a weekend of home leave. It's a common practice to help the prisoner start to adjust back into family life. He should have had a number of such visits but they held them back and it was a mixed blessing. It was more upsetting than reassuring, in fact.

The day after his weekend of home leave he was put into a double cell. Again he went on hunger strike and was brought before the governor who negotiated with him.

'He said I could go onto B3 Landing and get full privileges,' he says, as he swills the sink. 'That meant full association with other prisoners, use of the games room and telly at night. But I'd have to double up. I said, "What else?" He said I could go onto A3 Landing with no privileges and I'd be locked up every night from five till the next morning but I'd be in a single cell. I said that'll do me. I was in a bad way when Elsa came to visit with a doctor I was told the Communist Party had recommended and he told me to take the sedative I'd been prescribed. I knew it was only given to "awkward" prisoners but I was desperate and I trusted him. What a lemon.'

'What was it like, this sedative? What did it taste like?'

He turns his head to take me in for a moment, and moves to lift his shirt off the bed. He moves like a badly drawn cartoon in small, jerky gestures, as his arm finds the sleeve holes and he pushes his hands through. He gets stuck with the second sleeve and the shirt is hanging limp over one shoulder and half covering his back as he tries to find it.

I walk over and help him find the second sleeve, trying to block out the feeling that I'm dressing a giant child. He gives an embarrassed laugh that isn't really a laugh at all. I don't button up the shirt for him, I can't.

'It tasted like any other medicine. It tasted green.'

'And what was the effect?'

'I don't know.'

'What do you mean you don't know?'

'They called it the liquid cosh. It knocked you out.'

He's got most of the buttons done up now but he gives up on the top three and reaches for his padded jacket. I'm expecting a repeat of the one-sleeve performance but the jacket is more accommodating and he finds his way into it on his own.

'When I wasn't on work duty I'd sleep in my cell. I'd walk around like a zombie. Everything was muffled like it was happening through cotton wool. I walked slow. My mouth was dry all the time so I couldn't speak. But I never had any thoughts to speak anyway. If someone asked me a question I'd have to force the words out and they came out like I was drunk. Slurred.'

'Like you do now sometimes.'

'Aye.'

He moves back to sit on the edge of the bed but instead of lowering himself down he falls backwards. The mattress is soft and he bounces a couple of times before he becomes still. He looks up at me through those eyebrows and I sit in the wooden chair. In the clouded mirror of the wardrobe we look like two ghosts in a darkened room.

'What work did you do in that state?'

'I'd been with the building works department but they took me off that work for safety reasons when I went on the medicine.'

'What did they make you do instead?'

'I had to pack Ludo chips into plastic bags.'

'Fucking hell.'

'I was lucky.'

'How do you mean?'

'I worked at a table opposite another fellah. He'd get a big box of Ludo chips and he'd have to sort them into smaller boxes of the different colours. They were red, blue, green, yellow. When he'd finished they'd take the four little boxes to the far end of the workshop and tip them all into the big box. Then they'd give him the big box back and he'd start all over again.'

'Didn't it drive you mad?'

'I didn't know what was going on. Later they moved me on to making toy abacuses.'

'A promotion, was it?'

He laughs.

'Was everyone doing that kind of work?'

'It was that kind of workshop. No one was the full shilling. I made those for a few days before I realised I had to stop taking the drugs.'

We look at each other for a moment. I need a fag but I know he hates it so I'm not going to smoke in his bedroom. I can see his face stiffening and his hand is shaking in his lap.

'And that's when this started?'

'Not long after, yeah.'

'Cup of tea?'

'Aye, go on.'

I go down the stairs and put on a pan of water. I wish I smoked normal cigarettes because I can't roll this one fast enough.

When the tea is made Dad is standing outside on the veranda overlooking the lake. He is standing stiffly with his back against the wall but his head and shoulders are slumped forward.

'Push me back, will you?'

Putting the two mugs of tea down on the parapet, I push his shoulders hard. His muscles are all contracted in a spasm and pushing is almost impossible. I try to push him by the forehead instead but he groans angrily so I stop and go back to the shoulders. If I push a little bit at a time and leave short breaks in between I can move him slowly, incrementally, into an upright position. I stop when his shoulders are flush with the wall and decide to leave his head, which is already at a better angle anyway.

'Can you drink your tea?'

'Behave yourself.'

'You're not going to let it go to waste, are you?'

He laughs. I can see it in his eyes and hear the rumble of it in his chest although there's no trace of it on his face. But I know it's there, just as I know the rest of my dad is in there somewhere.

'So you want to go back home tomorrow then?'

'Aye.'

'That's all right. I'm nearly out of questions anyway.'

'Spanish Inquisition.'

'Just a son's fascination with his fabulous father.'

There is a smile in there somewhere. I can read the signs.

Snowed under

Steven Evans and Rob Jones used to call my dad Captain Fantastic. They'd ask questions about how he was doing and what he was up to in jail. I used to smile at the name at first, but as the months then the years went by and the date of his release got closer and closer, it was like the Shrewsbury Pickets had become somebody else's story, one that had gone on for too long. I was nearly fifteen and wanted my own life.

MPs used to visit Mum, and I'd have to make tea and listen to them going on about 'the latest developments'.

He was getting charged for stupid things. For sitting on his bed when a screw came into the cell – an extra week in prison. For being on the wrong landing – an extra week in prison. For taking too long at the washbasin – an extra week in prison. For not making his bed in the prescribed manner – an extra week in prison. For returning verbal abuse to a screw – an extra week in prison.

It was getting so bad that MPs were asking questions in the House of Commons on a regular basis. I looked at the MPs sitting in our house, and I put on the right face. But inside I was thinking, 'Why don't you do something instead of just whingeing about it?' It seemed that the workers couldn't do anything, union leaders couldn't do anything and even MPs couldn't do anything, so why didn't we all just shut up and give in? It got on my nerves talking about it all the time.

Then Mum got really sick and tired and had to go into hospital. This meant us kids had to go into care. I said I wanted to stay with my new friend, Steve Jones, instead.

Steve came from Liverpool to Denbigh because his parents were divorced and his mum had married a farmer. Their farm was up past the Denbigh Moors, about an hour away by bus, and I'd been out to visit him a couple of times. I liked it there. Better than a foster-home or an orphanage anyway.

I told my mum that Steve had asked his mum and she said it was all right. So my mum said all right and then we asked Steve's mum and she said all right as well. The next day Mum went into hospital and I visited her after school or in the lunch break.

She was in a bed in a public ward and looked tired and haggard, but she always smiled when I went to see her. They were giving her drugs and electro-shock therapy. She said it was making her feel better and that she'd be out soon.

I wanted to care but I just couldn't any more. It was like everyone in my family was sick or sad or just annoying. I wanted to stay on Steve's farm for ever and just forget about them all.

Steve's dad was a giant and he didn't say much. His mum was good-looking for a mum and she talked like a bird, little trilling sentences edged with worry and concern. It was easy being around them because they were both so busy.

Steve and I had to do jobs around the farm like milking the cows before the sun came up, putting logs into the electric saw for the fire and cleaning out the stables. We were allowed to take the shotgun out into the fields and fire into the trees at crows.

When it wasn't raining up there in the mountains it was snowing, so the ground was always deep with mud when it wasn't frozen in the rutted patterns from the fifty cows that traipsed through the farmyard twice a day. We'd wade through this rich mix of mud and cow pats to get to the stables and you'd laugh out loud because you'd nearly fall over with every step and have to drag your wellies out of the ooze with a plop that sometimes left your boot behind.

One night Steve's dad took us down narrow country lanes to the far side of the farm. He drove really fast in the pitch-black darkness and turned the headlights off as we screamed. Another time he let us hang onto the tailboard of the pick-up truck while he took us across the fields to help herd some sheep. Then the tailboard fell off and we both woke up out of a blackout and saw him calmly fixing the truck.

When the snows came they were heavy and fell to about two feet deep all over the place. You could wade up to the highest point of the farm and see nothing but white hills, almost invisible against a pinkish, grey-white sky, and you couldn't help shouting out with the joy that came up from your belly and had to get out.

One Saturday we took our fishing rods and we walked all the way to Brennig Dam on the Denbigh Moors. On the way there we dug our heels into the catseyes in the middle of the road to scoop out the little bits of glass to see how they worked. When we got to the dam where we were going to fish for pike we left the road and made our way through the snow. We fished for a couple of hours and caught some small pike that were just about big enough to cook. Then we decided to head back.

As we retraced our steps, the clouds came down and the fog was so thick we could barely see. We walked for about an hour until we rediscovered our own tracks in the snow. By then it was getting dark. I told Steve the story of *The Hound of the Baskervilles* and wished I hadn't started it before I'd got halfway through. We fell into the snow and made the shape of our bodies and then pissed where the heads were to make eyes.

Eventually we got back to the road and walked up to the pub at the top and ordered two pints, which they wouldn't give us, so we called his dad who came to fetch us but didn't say anything all the way home. I gutted the pike, Mrs Jones grilled them and we ate them. They were delicious.

Mum was out of hospital after just two weeks. Her smile was sort of hollow and she couldn't look at us without tears coming into her eyes.

I felt really bad about wanting to live on Steve Jones's farm for ever, and I tried to make her glad to have come home. I brewed loads of tea and told the kids to behave or at least to be quiet. I asked her to teach me yoga. She liked that.

Everyone was always on about our dad but nobody ever really thought about our mum.

Black Forest

Because Dad was a communist and in prison for picketing, some other countries, like East Germany, thought he was great. That's why were invited to spend our Christmas holiday there.

We were collected from Berlin airport by a chauffeur in a long black limousine. We drove through the Black Forest and we all made comments about the famous gateau. There were no jokes about the Germans until Andy and me got into our hotel room in a skiing resort, and we only did that after we'd checked the fruit bowl and the bedside lamps for bugs.

I don't know how he did it but our Chris made loads of German friends. He was forever tearing round the hotel corridors chasing girls, and they'd squeal with delight as he caught them and hurled them to the ground.

We had our own table in the hotel restaurant and we ate fried meat with breadcrumbs on it at every meal. The other guests would watch us with a kindly but distant interest and on Christmas morning there was a flurry of activity behind the enormous Christmas tree as hotel staff and our translator approached our table with a load of presents.

I learned to ski badly and once managed to stay upright for more than a hundred metres. But I couldn't turn, or stop at the bottom of the slope, which led straight onto a busy roadway. Right in my path was a small boy aged about three years old. To his mother's horror, all I could do was pick him up and carry him with me into the road. The traffic was slow-moving in a black and white scene of imminent disaster and to save us both I threw myself sideways and skidded to halt on the very edge of the road. The mother and other holidaymakers rushed up to us and whipped the startled little boy out of my arms. The laughter that followed was polite but relieved.

Andy and me spent a lot of time wandering through the Black Forest, which was incredibly beautiful like a black and white photograph with a thick rich smell of sap and soil, and a little strange, with whispers of *Hansel and Gretel*. We'd also spend time watching men playing bar billiards. Each time they'd drop the black billiard they'd roar, 'Hitler Kaput!'

It became clear to Mum that all of the other guests in the resort were government people 'relishing the privileges of the regime'. She said it was like we were on the flip side of our own life back home. I stopped enjoying it so much after she said that.

When we got back to Wales I unpacked my suitcase and noticed that all of my jeans and some of my other clothes were gone. I told Mum we'd been robbed but she said no, she'd given them to the maid who cleaned our rooms for her children.

Speed-training

Sawing a nick through the brass fittings at both ends of the fibreglass drain–cleaning pole that had been my fishing rod, I flexed a piece of baling twine to make the bow. The arrows were made from sections of electric conduit piping with a groove in one end for the string and a jagged, severed end for the arrowhead. Together they made a fantastic weapon and I used trees and telegraph poles for target practice.

Then one day, after I'd let Andy use the bow a few times to his great delight, I told him that it was time for him to learn about 'the need for speed'.

He looked at me for a moment and we both waited for what I meant to sink in. He started shaking his head. 'No, Nick, I don't want to do that, no.'

I wore a firm and regretful expression and let my lips fall into my dad's thin smile as I fitted the arrow to the bow and drew the string back with the grooved end. We were far out in the middle of the field and it was as far for him to run home as it was for him to run behind the nearest tree. I started counting down from twenty. By the time I'd got to a slow eighteen he knew I was serious and he bolted.

Keeping my counting measured and loud so he could hear, I lifted the weapon into the air and aimed over his rapidly receding head. When I got to number one I loosed the arrow.

Almost at once I regretted it. I could see his little body running as fast as he could over the rough terrain and could hear him whimpering as he ran. I could also see in the first moments of the arrow's flight that it was going to hit him. Panicking, I yelled, 'Move to the side, move to the side!'

He moved to one side but then he moved back to the other, which brought him straight back into the arrow's trajectory.

It struck him solidly between the shoulder blades and I felt a spasm of vomit before I dropped the bow and legged it over the field to where he was lying.

He was crying when I dropped to my knees next to him and there was nothing I could say to let him know how sorry I was and how stupid I felt.

'Fuck off! Just leave me alone, will you! I only want to be your brother. What's wrong with you?'

As Andy headed back to the house I stayed on my knees, twisting the improvised arrow in my hands and listening to his gradually receding sobs.

What *was* wrong with me?

Bob

One day after school I changed into my tracksuit and was running home instead of catching the bus when a car pulled up next to me. It was the old battered blue Citroën Dyane that was driven by our art teacher, Bob Carvel.

He leaned over the passenger seat and rolled down the window, his smoking pipe held in place between gritted teeth. 'What are you doing, young Master Warren?'

I didn't break my stride but something in his attitude annoyed me so I picked up the pace. 'I'm running home, what does it look like?'

'You know real exercise comes in the form of manual labour.'

'Yeah? Well, I haven't got any manual labour, have I? So this is my best option.'

'Good point, Warren. Good point. Come up to my place this Saturday and we'll see what we can do about that. There'll be wages involved.'

Then he started to pull away from me and shouted out of the window, 'I'll give you directions after class on Thursday!'

As soon as he had driven around the bend I stopped running and started grinning. I liked Bob Carvel a lot, he was a cool teacher. I also liked the look of the blonde girl in the brown school uniform that had sat in the back of the car throughout our conversation beaming at me with undisguised interest.

St Christopher

I used to hitchhike the 10 miles to Bob Carvel's place on the days when he couldn't collect me in his car. It was easy but unpredictable so I decided I needed a bike.

I told Chris I'd make one for him too and together we went to the nearby dump to scrounge for parts. We got most of the things we needed and only had to buy new chains, a few spokes, brake leads and pads. Both bikes were wobbly and not especially safe, but we were happy to race around the village on them and got through a fair few shoes in the braking processes.

Chris came home from school one day looking fed up. There'd been a Road Safety Day at the junior school in Henllan and they all had to ride their bikes through this obstacle course. The Road Safety Officer had said he wasn't even allowed to attempt the course because his bike was a death trap.

I longed for a new racer like a lot of my friends had but that was out of the question. Mum was still in a bit of a state and requests like that just made her upset.

One morning before school I was racing down the road on my bike to get food for breakfast and had to be quick because everybody had slept late and Mum was shouting and bawling, trying to get the kids dressed, and they weren't allowed to go without eating. I got to the crossroads at the bottom of the hill. There was never any traffic that early in the morning and I didn't want to slow down and lose impetus because I had to climb up the hill on the other side to get to the shop.

I saw the car in the corner of my eye and braked to no effect and smashed into the side of it. I rolled along the tarmac and came to rest against the grey stone steps leading up to the post office.

The car was an Alfa Romeo. The driver got me inside and asked where I lived. I felt sick but most of it was already up and out on the road. Sitting in a bucket seat of pain in the car, I kept my eyes fixed on the swinging St Christopher pendant hanging from the rear-view mirror.

Mum was hysterical and the poor bloke did everything he could to calm her down but she was having none of it. He offered to take me to the hospital in Denbigh but I said that I was fine and eventually she let the man go and thanked him.

I had to spend the rest of the day in bed. She'd come in every now and then, hold up fingers and shine a torch in my eyes.

Later that afternoon, when the other kids were back from school, I got up because of the boredom and asked Mum if I could go and fetch my bike from down the road. It was as if I'd put a bomb under her. She leaped out of the chair and started smacking me around the head and screaming that I could have died and was I mad and I was never, ever going to see that bike again as long as I lived.

Chris moved slowly out of the room, but she ran past him to the back yard, picked up his bike and threw it over the wall into the back neighbour's garden.

We all looked at her in amazement. The neighbour was a specialist doctor and he had a beautiful Spanish wife, but we never really spoke to them and they were both very quiet, unassuming people. The image of Chris's homemade bike flying over the wall into their flower bed coupled with the look on our faces was too much for Mum and she started crying with laughter.

She gave Andy and me an embarrassing hug, then Diane, Katy and Chris came to get a bit of it, too. She kept laughing and crying and saying, 'My children' over and over again, and I stood in the centre of it all wondering how long I should leave it before I built another bike.

An invitation to artists

One day Bob Carvel announced to the class that he had 'gained permission from the school's board of governors to take a group of worthwhile and mature young students to an artists' retreat for three nights'.

Bob was a popular teacher. The idea of going on an art trip with such a man was irresistible to everyone in the class.

There were permission forms to be collected at the end of class and to be returned with 'authentic parental signatures' by the end of the week for those interested.

I told Mum it was compulsory but that she had to sign an indemnity form in case I died. I made it into a joke because the only way I'd get it through was if I made it so ridiculous not to sign that she'd feel like a freak.

She looked at the form for too long. She was sitting in her special rocking chair wearing a big floral skirt and a turtleneck sweater of my dad's. (She'd started wearing all of my dad's clothes recently and this annoyed me because I first started wearing his stuff and now she was copying me.)

'Who is this *loco in parentis*?'

'Bob Carvel. You've met him. I work up at his place doing building at the weekends and holidays. He's a very responsible person. He's got a beard, three kids and a wife, and he smokes a pipe. There's nothing to worry about.'

'And where will you be staying?'

'In a tent with Neil and Bugsy. It's their tent. They've already got it. We don't have to buy one.'

'That's not what I meant.'

'It's a farmhouse in the mountains somewhere. I think it's near Llanwrst or Llansomething. There's a lake, but it's shallow and I can swim.'

'Girls?'

'What do you mean?'

'You know very well what I mean.'

'Some girls are going as well, yeah. Everyone's going, Mum. The whole class is going!'

'Let me see your lotus.'

'Now?'

'Now. For fifteen minutes.'

Suppressing everything that wanted to come rushing up inside me, I sat down opposite Mum and folded myself into the lotus position. I concentrated on my breathing and felt myself become limp and centred. With my eyes closed and my breathing easy and shallow, the household noises fell away to shadows of sound and I pictured the image of a lake lapping against a gentle shore. In the far distance I could hear Mum's regular movements as the springs of her rocking chair contracted and relaxed, and the other kids came and went with their medley of requests and comments. None of it touched me.

Then I opened my eyes and looked into those of my mother.

She glanced at her watch and nodded. 'Now ask me again.'

'Please, Mum, I'd like to go on this art trip.'

'You're a good boy. Of course you can go. Get me a pen.'

Holy water

I'm in the house doing art homework. It's a portrait and I'm sick and tired of looking in the mirror. I go downstairs and I look around. Diane does one of her big laughs and runs away when I ask her to pose. Katy says no, flatly. Andy's out with his mates and then there's Chris. He's young but he's up for it.

I take him up to my room. I tell him to strip down to his undies, put him into the lotus position on the floor and tell him he's got to sit still. He's only seven but he takes it seriously. I start drawing and then painting. He's so still he looks as though he isn't breathing. I tell him to relax and ask him what's going on.

He talks almost without moving his lips. 'I'm in trouble with the church.'

'What do you mean?'

'You know in that bit outside the church, the place where you can sit down before you walk through the graveyard?'

'Yeah?'

'I was there and I saw someone had written horrible things.'

'What horrible things?'

'Horrible things!'

'Okay, don't worry about it. Then what?'

'I thought I should get rid of the horrible things that were there so I did a wee on the words.'

'Okay … Yeah?'

'I thought the wee would wash the words. But it didn't.'

'That's okay. You did your best.'

'But the vicar came out of the church and he thought I wrote the words and I was weeing on the church.'

'But did you explain?'

'I ran away.'

'Jesus, Chris!'

'Now the vicar's after me.'

'Listen, mate. Don't worry about it. The vicar doesn't know who you are. None of us have ever been in that church and none of us is ever going in either.'

'Everyone knows who we are.'

'I tell you what. If he comes round I'll take care of it, all right?'

'All right, Nick.'

'But you've got to keep still.'

And he did. For about two hours he didn't move a muscle and when I'd finished my homework I had to pick him up and unravel him slowly to get the blood moving again.

The vicar never came round.

The helping hand

We'd been talking about it for weeks before we actually did it. We brought special clothes in our gym bags and practised what we were going to say. When the day came we rushed through lunch and set off just after one o'clock in our civvies with our stomachs churning.

We had heard that the best place to order and receive your first under-age drink was from a pub called the Hand off the roundabout on Henllan Road. It was all about attitude. Neil, Johnny Fish and I slowed our steps the closer we got, then I said, 'Fuck it' and strode onwards, pushing open the door.

Nobody turned round to look at us and nobody stopped talking and the smell was fantastic and men just sat around reading the paper or watching the telly and in the corner you could see 'the entertainments section' with video games and a jukebox and a cigarette machine and a one-armed bandit that we called 'the tettin' and a dartboard.

Indicating that corner to Neil and Johnny, I walked up to the bar. My hand was in my pocket and I was afraid that the sweat of my palm had turned the notes into sopping rags of illegality. Pretending to be my grandad, I leaned against the bar, put a blank smile of greeting on my face, dropped my voice and spoke casually. 'Can I have some change for the Space Invader? And three pints of bitter please, mate.'

The barman didn't even blink. He took my fiver, put a glass in place behind the counter and pulled a lever to pour the first pint. Then he punched the cash register and handed me a fist full of coins. I didn't say anything because my mouth was so dry but I silently looked at the change in my hand and calculated that the notes and the coins added up to five pounds minus the cost of three beers.

Turning to Neil and Johnny, I had to glance away almost immediately because they looked too hysterical. They both had wide eyes and nervous expressions and they looked about ten years old. I nearly exploded with a big snotty laugh.

The barman put the three frothy beers on the counter, walked back to his stool by the cash register and picked up his newspaper like nothing had happened.

We could hardly look at each other. We all just stared at our beers and then in unison we picked them up and took that first big gulp.

We nodded sagely as if to say 'not a bad pint' and put them back on the table for the briefest time before we picked them up again.

Next it was Johnny's turn to get the round in, then Neil's and by the time I was back up at the bar we were in that special place of brewer's heaven where the whole world is your friend, everything is funny and life is truly, surprisingly good.

Running shoes

One day I came home from school and asked Mum if I could make another bike. She said no way. I looked at her in her rocking chair. She was wearing another hippy skirt and writing another letter to some MP or Trades Council. There was a pile of letters on the floor at her feet ready for envelopes. She wrote about ten letters a day and had done since the beginning. The futility of it irritated me.

'Why don't you save up the money you get for the odd jobs you do on the farms and at Carvel's and buy a proper bike instead of spending it all on beer?' she said.

'I don't spend it all on beer!'

'And cigarettes.'

'You don't know what you're talking about!'

'Don't you dare speak to me like that. You will treat me with respect!'

'Respect is something you have to earn, not something you can demand.'

She rocketed forward, spurred by the momentum of the rocking chair, and in one movement she had her shoe off her foot and was heading for me with a look of unbridled fury. I ran.

I flung the front door open and raced over the road to the car park. I could hear her bare feet slapping the ground behind me. Reaching the far side of a parked car, I looked over my shoulder and couldn't believe she was still chasing me! I thought she would have given up on the street because she was always worried about what the neighbours thought.

We ran around the car three times before she slowed to a stop and suddenly laughed. It was as if she'd suddenly seen how funny this must look: a middle-aged, bare-foot hippy woman with a Chinese slipper in her hand, chasing a uniformed schoolboy.

'What are we doing? Look at us!'

Still shocked and angry, it took me longer to come down. She stopped laughing and looked at me over the bonnet of the car. 'Your dad's coming home soon. Maybe very soon, in a couple of months. You can ask him for a bike.'

'You won't tell him I smoke?'

'No, I won't. But you better not let him find out.'

'Fair enough.'

'Respect?'

'Respect.'

One weekend

Dad got a weekend home visit to get used to the idea of being out. He should have had loads of home visits but they forgot to tell him. We went to bed on Saturday night with him in the house and we spent Sunday around Henllan. I took him across the fields and into the woods, and showed him my secret places and the tricks that Bruce could do. I talked and he'd say, 'Oh aye, yeah.'

I could see that his mind was elsewhere but I didn't care because he was right there next to me, moving around in my world.

Going to sleep that Sunday night and saying, 'Night, Dad!' made a bubble of joy in my gut that kept me awake for ages. I took that feeling deep into my dreams. The next morning when I woke up I had the opposite feeling. He had a tiny little bag packed and it was already lying on the floor next to the front door. When he tried to go I couldn't help myself. It was like somebody had turned a switch and I fell into a long and breathless weeping fit that I couldn't stop as he tried to explain why he had to go back for another six months.

Freedom

Glan Gerrionedd

Released

Dad and I walk along the edge of the forest through thinning fir trees on a muddy path to get to a small beach area at the lake's edge. The path is slippery but there are trunks to lean against as we proceed slowly onwards. He's not thrilled at the idea of this little outing but I have insisted.

The sky is a dull aluminium of low cloud, like the underbelly of a dead fish, and the tree trunks are black with the moisture rolling off the lake. Birds in the higher branches mark our progress with reports back and forth, as we mulch moist earth and crack dead twigs under our boots.

We arrive at the spot and take seating positions on a rock and a felled tree trunk. We let our breathing fall shallow and I reach into my pocket for tobacco. The lake is quiet now with only the smallest waves lapping at the silted shore. It is the colour of pulped newsprint.

'So what happened in the end?' I ask Dad.

'I came off the medicine and felt like crap. About three days later I was writing a petition to the Home Office for early release on compassionate grounds. Your mum was still very ill and I wanted to get home. A lot of other lads were released for lesser reasons, but I was a dangerous trade unionist and so the application was denied by Jenkins. It was while I was writing the petition that I noticed I couldn't move the fingers of my right hand. The whole of my right side was stiff.'

Picking up a dead twig, I dig my thumbnail under the bark and start to peel it off. 'And then?'

'Leicester was a maximum security prison and one screw did everything he could to wind me up. This one time he was looking after a load of cons on a building job and when he saw me passing he left the cons on their own with a load of extending ladders – escape equipment! – so he could give me some lip. I put in a charge of harassment and negligence. Normally a charge like that was dealt with on the same day or soon afterwards but I didn't hear anything about it for three weeks. Then I was called into the governor's office.'

'What happened?'

'Governor told me I was up for a meeting with the visiting magistrates next day to discuss the issue of returning my lost remission – or what was left of it. He said he would recommend in my favour and there was a good chance they'd go with it and I'd be released. That meant I could be out the day after. The only problem was they couldn't release me while there was a charge still pending. So I was looking at another three days or three months inside. Every charge I'd ever laid against the screws got covered up by the Home Office and there was no reason to think this one would go any differently. So I squared things with the governor and agreed to drop the charges.'

'And did he keep his word?'

'The morning after the visiting magistrates met I was told to get my gear and I was out on the street. It was the fifth of August nineteen seventy-six. There was nobody there. I stood on the empty street for a while then made my way off to the train station.'

In the silence that follows I grip the twig hard in both hands and twist. I revel in the sensation of the bark crumbling to leave a yellowed, bone-coloured digit of wood in my hands. I let the pieces of bark fall to the earth at my feet.

'Nicky?'

'Yeah?'

'I've had enough now, mate.'

'I know.'

'It's about a four-hour drive, isn't it?'

'Yeah.'

'Shall we make a move then?'

'Okay.'

I pick up a rock and lean back, throwing it far out into the lake. It makes an unspectacular splash out in the mist. I picture it falling through the depths to mingle with the slate shingle on the stony, loamy bottom for ever.

I bring the Beetle as close as possible to the farmhouse and pop the bonnet to start loading our luggage and supplies. Dad has managed to carry his own little canvas bag and lobs it into the boot at the front of the car and then climbs into the passenger seat. He watches the lake with a steady eye that shifts only when I pass by with more kit to be packed up.

'Comfy are you? Don't worry about me, Dad, I'll pack everything up!'

He doesn't wear his watch any more because it irritates his skin, but he keeps it in a pocket and he pulls it out now to check the time with a smile. It's a beautiful gold Omega that the lads bought for him for brokering a great deal when he was a shop steward on a site years ago.

I can see he's impatient to get going. I stroll back to the farmhouse and pack the last box of tinned food, sugar and condiments, placing it on the table near the front window which overlooked the veranda and the lake. I roll a cigarette and smoke it gazing over the lake.

I take a final drag, flick the butt into the wet undergrowth and head down to the car. I spark up the Beetle, lean over to fasten Dad's seatbelt and we set off. This time I'll drive round the other side of the lake where there are no gates between here and the open road.

It's after eleven in the morning and the sun is warming the clouds, turning them translucent with the sweat that comes before a light rain.

Dad is silent in the passenger seat, flexing his fingers to keep them mobile. I push a tape in and turn up the volume. It's loud enough to give a background sound for me to focus on but low enough for conversation, should any arise.

At a T-junction I take the opportunity to give him the once-over. He looks relaxed and content.

'Glad to be going home, are you?'

'Aye.'

We pull onto a main road and I floor the accelerator. The engine roars out a throaty rumble through the small hole in the exhaust pipe, loud enough to drown out the possibility of further conversation. He is toying with his watch for a while, rolling the wristband through his fingers. He suddenly leans over and hands it to me.

'Here you go, mate. You can have this. Thanks for everything.'

I feel the weight of the watch in my hand and there's a warm smile flooding up from inside me. I check the rear-view and then turn to him beaming. 'Hey – thanks, Dad.'

'You're all right. Now slow down. There's no rush.'

Yellow ribbon

I was fifteen when Dad came out of prison in August 1976, and it was fantastically exciting to have him back, at least for a while.

On the day he came home Mum tied a yellow ribbon around the trunk of an elderflower bush in the field just opposite our house. There was song on the radio about this man who was coming home after 'three long years' and Mum thought it'd be a great idea to copy the song. The ribbon was long but it wasn't very thick so if you looked at it from the house you could hardly see it. When Dad got home later that day it took ages before he spotted it and we had to explain what it was all about because he didn't know the song.

A few weeks after his return the whole family were invited for a holiday down in Margate by one of the unions. I didn't want to go. I'd made plans to go on a caravan holiday with Paul Smith and his family.

We'd already spent a week on holiday with Dad in Blackpool as guests of Bill Cross and his family in their guesthouse paid for by the Blackpool Trades Council. It had been a great holiday. I remember the joke shops where you could buy stink bombs and fart cushions, and that you were never more than two minutes away from a fish and chip shop. All the grass was mowed, there were flower beds everywhere, everything was neat and tidy, and there were parks and playgrounds where you could go and play for free.

Dad wasn't the same in Blackpool. It was as though he was looking over our heads or listening with one ear and thinking about other things all the time. It was the same now he had come home from prison for ever. I tried to talk to him but he'd listen and then focus his eyes on me as if he was trying to work out who I was. He didn't seem to be interested in what I had to say and everything seemed to just remind him of another thing he had to do.

One day I showed him one of my paintings from school and he looked at it for a minute. 'That's nothing,' he said eventually. 'There was this fellah inside who could do a painting in under an hour and you could look at it for days and find new things to see every time. He used to sell them to the screws for tobacco and whisky.'

'Yeah? That's great, Dad.'

'What's up, mate?'

'Nothing. I'm just going to my room. Listen, is it all right if I don't come with you to Margate? I'm going to the coast with a friend of mine. We planned it ages ago.'

'Up to you, mate.'

The morning they left I went over the road to the elderflower bush with Bruce. The yellow ribbon was all dirty from the rain and the dust after so many weeks. I cut it down and let it go in the wind.

Political enlightenment

One Saturday morning, Mick Farley and a few lads from the Workers Revolutionary Party came to visit from Wigan and they brought me a brand new bike. It was bright yellow, made by 'Sun' and it had ten gears with a Shimano changer. I couldn't believe it.

Mum had told these lads that I wanted a bike for my birthday but that she couldn't afford one and they had organised a collection on several sites around Wigan. After unpacking it, checking it over and thanking them a thousand times, I went for a spin around the village.

Along our road past the Miserable Ords. Down the road to the junction by the post office. Up the hill past the shops where I bought our breakfast and tea. Past the council estate with their pebble-dashed houses. Past Plas Meifod, the new estate where Paul Smith lived. Along the Garn Woods end where Sharon the Flirt lived with her angry husband. Down Garn Hill where the manor was. Past the hospice for old people where the lawns were like a bowling green. Then up the final slope of Ty Coch street to our house where Andy was waiting with a watch to clock my time. 'Eight minutes and twenty-two seconds, Nick!'

I rushed into the house to tell Dad and the lads, but when I got into the lounge and started talking, Dad put up his hand. 'We're in a meeting, Nicky. We'll talk about the bike later, all right?'

They spent the best part of the day together and when they left I said thanks again. I liked them a lot for thinking to do such a thing.

'That was a big chat,' I said to Dad later. 'What did you talk about?'

'The politics of the campaign.'

'But they're Trotskyites, aren't they?'

'Aye.'

'I thought communists didn't like Trotskyites.'

'Do you know how much work these fellahs did on the campaign?'

'Everyone did their bit, didn't they?'

'These fellahs did a bit more from what I can see.'

'Does that mean you're going to become a Trotskyite then?'

'Give it a rest, will you, Nicky?'

I knew what it was like to lose old friends and make new ones, so I didn't push it. Dad was still waiting for his 'debriefing' from the Communist Party but they were keeping a very low profile and it was getting on his nerves. He was writing a pamphlet about the case and the Communist Party was sheepish about getting involved. They wouldn't help him write it, wouldn't help get it printed and then wouldn't review it in the party newspaper, the *Morning Star*, until he pestered them for a few months. It was called, *Shrewsbury: Whose Conspiracy?* And it looked as though he was the only one who wanted to ask this question and push the thing through to what he felt was its logical conclusion.

'I want a retrial with the state in the dock.'

Mum wasn't happy. 'Let it go, Dennis.'

'No chance.'

Leaving the room before the conversation turned into another row, I looked through the shed for some oil for the gears of my new bike. Trotskyites were all right in my book.

The hopper

Leslie Hopper was a year older than me but she was like a grown-up woman. And she was friendly. I'd sometimes visit her brother at his home where we'd listen to records and eat Jaffa Cakes, but the visits only really ever came alive for me when his sister came home.

He could see I was interested in her and he didn't like it. He told me plenty of times that she was already going out with an older man called Peter Rabbit who had a Bowie knife and drove a Honda 250cc motorbike.

I never believed that somebody called Peter Rabbit could be paired with someone called Leslie Hopper, but the poetry of throwing a Warren into the mix seemed too good to be true. I made a big deal of sharing this joke with Leslie one day during lunch and to my amazement she liked the idea and said she'd come and visit me the next weekend.

'We can got for a walk, if you like.'

That Saturday, at eleven o'clock, I met her off the bus at the end of our road. I'd been waiting for her since nine-thirty, kicking up stones, scuffing poppies around the church cemetery, and practising opening remarks. When she stepped down from the bus I nearly burst into a fit of giggles because I was so nervous and excited but I managed to keep myself under control. She smiled when she saw me and then kissed me on the mouth. Just like that. Straight away. I must have looked very pleased because she laughed, then took my hand and asked where we were going.

We walked right out of the village and turned left onto a footpath, which took a long route back into the village further on. We stopped at a gate overlooking a field of tall grass. I'd worked that field last year as a hay-baler for Foxhall Farm and I would do so again this year. I chatted about the work and the wages.

'Can we go in?' she asked.

We were barely into the field before she pulled me off the track into the grass and lay on her back. Fumbling with her clothes, I unleashed her freckled, fleshy breasts, she loosened her jeans and I dragged them off her, and she undid me and pulled me out and guided me into her.

I stammered about a rubber johnny and she said she was on the pill and then all of ancient pagan natural hell broke loose and it was over within minutes.

Rolling over, I lay beside her, staring up at grey clouds racing by in a pale-blue sky framed by tall grasses dancing in the breeze. I was smiling like a fool.

She looked at me and said I'd made her lips bleed from kissing her so hard. I was very sorry. I tried to look at her lip and into her eyes, but my gaze kept returning to her breasts, now nuzzling each other side by side as she leaned over towards me.

'You've done this before, haven't you?' she said.

'Yes,' I lied.

She wanted to know who with and mentioned the names of some likely candidates. I had to turn cowardly evasion into a moral position and told her that it was unfair to mention names.

She got a little moody after that but I was so happy that I just bulldozed her mood until it crumbled and we walked back into the village where I couldn't wait to get rid of her so I could go and tell Paul Smith.

Paul was about to go out for a drive up onto the moors with his older sister and I agreed to go with them.

We got out of the car and I dragged him to one side away from his sister so I could boast.

'I just did it! This afternoon! It was fantastic!'

We raced each other to the top of a hill stumbling over and through determined gorse bushes all the way. I ran with all my heart and stood at the summit, throwing my arms up and yelling at the wonderful indifference of fabulous Nature all around me.

Sinking

One day a reporter and a photographer from the *Morning Star* came round to do a piece on Dad. They talked for a little while but Dad was watching himself because a lot of what he felt these days about the Communist Party of Great Britain wasn't complimentary. His usual line was: 'They misled the campaign and bent and buckled and kowtowed to right-wing union leadership. They did everything to contain the movement and preserve their relationships with Labour rather than give a political organisational lead to the kind of mass action that would have got the job done.'

But on this day he was keeping his criticisms to a minimum because he was still finding evidence to support his theory and so he looked happy and relaxed when he posed in front of the kitchen sink and peeled a few potatoes for the camera.

Me and Mum watched from behind the photographer and

laughed into our hands because he'd never been big on domestic chores before he'd gone to prison. Mum whispered, 'Maybe he did learn something inside after all.'

Mum had changed a lot in the three years he'd been away and of course he had, too.

Mum had been very active in the Shrewsbury Defence Committee and had become intensely political through her speeches at rallies and her dealings with Labour MPs, Unionists, Socialist organisations and of course the media. But with Dad home she thought it was all over and they could get back to being a family.

Dad had different ideas. The political aspects of his trial and imprisonment had been the one deep and nourishing well that had sustained him throughout his prison term and he felt compelled to see it through to a full vindication of everything that he had stood for.

The hugs and kisses of the first few weeks soon gave way to extended silences in front of the TV and increasingly long separations as Dad attended political meetings all over the country. Within a few months the political animal that had been caged for so long was relishing the promise of action.

He'd been to see doctors about his increasing paralysis and speech impediment, and they prescribed pills to help his movements but nobody could pin it down and he started sharing Mum's tranquillisers before he got his own prescription.

The Comrades Arms

Dad told the Shrewsbury Defence Committee to petition the leader of the TUC to push for an inquiry into the whole Shrewsbury case. Len Murray agreed but all he did was write another letter to the prime minister.

They'd tried the same thing at the last two TUC conferences and Dad didn't think a letter was going to do it this year either. He wanted to go and speak at the TUC conference but, like Ricky before him, they didn't give him a chance.

Dad decided to go anyway and asked me to go with him. We drove up to Blackpool and went up to the conference centre, but they wouldn't let him in because he wasn't a delegate. It was embarrassing. Some of the other delegates were on his side and said, 'Do you know who this is?' But it didn't make any difference. I could see Dad was angry but he tried to shrug it off.

We went to a pub nearby. It was narrow pub with a long bar and just one door so you could see who came in and out. So many people in there kept coming up to Dad to shake his hand and ask if they could buy him a drink. They called him a hero, and some said they were ashamed because they hadn't managed to get him out. Dad said he knew everyone had done their bit and then he'd say why the shame was on the Labour government and the union leadership.

We were both standing at the bar just like Grandad said you should. I stood behind Dad most of the time unless someone recognised me or Dad introduced me. I felt great being there amidst the smoke and chat and laughing and shouting. Dad had one beer and he drank it very slowly, which drove me mad because I counted up and we could have had about thirty free pints. Dad bought me half a shandy and I got my own crisps.

Then this man came in. He was a big fellah and I recognised him as the man who came to our house and gave me his tie the day Dad was sent away. I smiled when he came up. But then he didn't shake Dad's hand, just told Dad that he was out of order blaming the leadership for his time in jail and he wasn't doing the movement any good.

Dad stuffed his hands in the pocket of his coat, rolled backwards and forwards on his feet and started saying why he thought what he did, but the big man just shook his head and walked away.

It was horrible. Dad laughed and dropped his head, then reached for his beer, which must have been warm and flat, and took a sip.

There must have been some important vote going on at the conference because just after that the pub started to empty. A few more people came up to Dad to thank him and offer to buy him a drink, but I couldn't get over the tie man. When he was in prison the important people wouldn't let him out, and now he was out the important people wouldn't let him in.

Dad pushed his warm beer across the bar and squared his shoulders. 'Come on, Nicky, let's go home.'

A pony's tale

In some ways Dad being out of jail didn't make much difference to our everyday lives. The house was still full of politics and Shrewsbury as he pursued his case around the country, trying to publicise the political consequences. I loved my dad but I saw Bob Carvel more often and I found him easier to talk to on some levels.

Anna Carvel had a big head for her body but she was gorgeous. She was like a pony. She was seventeen years old and moved through the world at a trot, frisking her long, tied-up blonde hair in sprays of gesture and enthusiasm. She had a forever smile that registered the pleasure she took from everything around her.

There was never a moment of doubt that she wanted me and even though it was a bit overwhelming in the beginning I soon gave in to it. This was partly helped by Bob himself, who obviously featured large in the emotional landscape of Anna and me and what might happen.

One Sunday I was working with him on his house. He had bought the property as a collection of sheds from a nearby farmer and they were living in a caravan on the land till the house was finished.

I was fitting a window frame into his kitchen. His kitchen was off the huge gallery space they called a lounge and it was high up because the land outside sloped from the front door to the west of the building.

Bob asked Anna to hold the ladder for me outside while he positioned himself inside the kitchen to receive the window frame.

Anna rushed into place with her usual enthusiasm and clung

on to the ladder with both hands before I'd even stepped onto it. I had to push myself past her to get onto the bottom rung of the ladder and instead of moving out of the way she pushed herself deeper into me, smiling broadly.

Later Bob lit his pipe and asked me to walk with him. I knew what was coming and had my 'honourable intentions' speech all worked out. He led me across to the small patch where he was growing his own pipe tobacco. He talked about tobacco farming for a while. It was interesting; everything Bob said was interesting.

Then he took me into a small stone shed and to show me the drying and curing processes.

'So, Warren?'

'Yeah?'

'Anna likes you.'

'Seems so, yeah.'

'And that's all right with me.'

'Right.'

'Good. Let's get some sealant on that frame, shall we?'

And that was it really. Even though Anna lived far away and went to a different school we saw each other every time I was working on her house and once she'd got her driving licence she'd drive through to see me on her way home.

But I always found her skittish enthusiasm a bit embarrassing in front of my friends and for a long time was torn by my own private joy of her and our public image together. It was difficult to be cool and detached with someone hanging off your lips and stroking your hair, and being cool and detached was a matter of life or death when you were sixteen.

She grew to understand this over the months we were together and one day she called me out of my house to walk with her on the football field opposite to tell me that it was over between us and she was going to college.

I cried as much because she was leaving as because she seemed so enthusiastic about our parting.

Soviet Union

Dad couldn't handle the conversational style of a family of five kids. We'd all changed a lot while he'd been away, and everybody had their own thoughts and ideas and wanted to be heard when they wanted to speak. Mum had somehow developed a way of fielding this but Dad never did. 'One at a time, one at a time!' he'd say.

When that happened we'd all quieten down for a while, but mostly it was because we had to take stock of this man, this stranger, and work out how he was going to fit into our lives. The other problem he had was that he was somehow deluded into thinking that his conversation carried more weight than any of ours.

He was in the lounge with Mum one day talking about how to deal with an invitation that had just arrived to visit the Soviet Union as guests of the state. He was talking about the difference between Socialism and Communism and she was wondering what they would need to wear when Christy came bounding in and started talking to Mum. Dad just raised his voice a little and continued his sentence but Mum put her hand up almost immediately and cut him short.

'Just a minute, Dennis. What is it, Christopher?'

Dad nearly hit the roof. 'I was talking!'

I was sitting on the sofa reading a book and looked up, intrigued to see how this was going to play out.

'Dennis, you know I can't ignore the children. It might be important.'

'Important? He's eight years old!'

'Exactly. And you're a grown man. Go on, Christopher.'

But Dad didn't hang around to hear what Christy had to say. He threw the invitation across the room and stormed out of the house without even glancing at his hair or taking a coat.

I knew Mum was right, but she was winding Dad up as well.

I also knew that Dad had overreacted.

What I didn't know was why.

Kissing Thatcher

One day my English teacher Philip Bennett bounced up to me while I was playing football in the playground and told me that there was going to be a mock election at the school and I should stand for Labour.

I wasn't enthusiastic. 'I can't stand for Labour because I don't believe in them any more.'

'Fine. That's all right. Stand for Independent Labour and talk about the changes you'd like to make!'

He was so animated by the idea that I couldn't look him in the face, but couldn't disappoint him either.

'All you've got to do is put up some posters and make some speeches in the form rooms. It's going to be a secret ballot and it'll be good for you to work out some of your thoughts.'

But I didn't have any thoughts. And most of all I didn't want to go into debates against the brainiest girl in the school, who was standing for the Tories, and less still her brainy boyfriend, who was standing for the Liberal Party. The thought of listening to their comfortable, well-measured slogans was more than I could stand.

'I've put your name up already. All you have to do is sign here and we'll be on!'

I signed a statement that said I would conduct myself honourably in what I hoped would be a vigorously fought but free and fair election for the fictional government of Denbigh High School and then I got on with my football game.

Word soon got out that I was standing for Independent Labour, and as nobody was standing for Labour it was a three-horse race. My friends would ask me what I was going to do about free condoms for the boys' toilets and could I see to it that our maths teacher, 'Bulldog', got moved to the position of groundsman.

But I also noticed that gangs of girls started giggling and whispering when I walked past. I liked this and tried out my campaign:

'Vote for me, girls, and I'll see you're all right.'

'Fuck off, wanker!'

After misjudging my popularity, I retreated to the back of

the running and adopted a silent campaign against my opposition. It has to be said that they ran a brilliant campaign. As well as posters everywhere boasting all sort of rhyming slogans, they also organised free discos and gave out badges at their 'rallies'. They also spoke extremely well. The Tory candidate held a meeting in the sixth-form common room and I stood at the back and watched for a while.

Elizabeth Morris was a tall, thin girl with the promise of a figure under a shock of blonde curls. She looked in total control as she stood on the teacher's desk at the front of the class flanked by her friends holding banners. She caught my eye and, like a real politician, tried to drag me into a debate.

'Does the honourable gentleman for Independent Labour honestly think that massive funding of a welfare state is going to provide the impetus for economic growth? This in an environment where it pays more to be a scrounger on the state than to take up the very many jobs that are ready and waiting to be done?'

It was very impressive. We all knew who Margaret Thatcher was because she had stolen our milk and this could have been her godchild addressing me. The crowd turned to face me expectantly.

'I think if a job's worth doing it's worth a decent wage – not the pocket money you're talking about,' I said.

The classroom erupted with cheers and applause, and I took my reddening face outside to remove myself from the onslaught of her response, which she was now bellowing over the roaring crowd.

My speech became a slogan that kids recited to me cheerfully in the corridors as they passed by. It was all I ever said and I only ever said it once. I didn't deserve to win.

I didn't pretend it had anything to do with my 'campaign'. It had everything to do with the fact that we lived in a Labour stronghold and the majority of voters had grown up in Labour lounges listening to their parents muttering Labour responses to the outpourings of the Tory media.

When the results were announced at assembly the day after the election, Elizabeth graciously approached me and took my hand.

'Congratulations, Nick.'

'I didn't deserve to win. You ran a better campaign.'

'Maybe we can discuss it sometime. After school.'

She said it in such a way that I knew she wasn't talking about pushing forward the frontiers of political science. Plus she was still holding my hand. All around us kids were flowing past, running for class in response to the school bell.

'I thought you were with Philip?'

'I was.'

I didn't really like her, but I couldn't help but be interested. I'd never thought of her as anything more than a posh swot who admired Thatcher. It felt weird to be holding her warm hand – and faintly treacherous.

'I'll see you outside the gate tonight then.'

I never told Dad about the election because I knew what he'd say – by working within the system of capitalist democracy I was just retarding the socialist revolution.

The Scottish play

Dad's pamphlet was printed and he thought people would be hammering the door down telling him to explain himself but nothing happened.

We took a family trip up to Scotland so Dad could visit a doctor in Edinburgh about his shakes, which were getting worse.

While we were there we had to have lunch with some big union man. He was a mountain who stood head and shoulders over Dad. He had a big red head with a few wisps of ginger hair, and his white shirt was stretched over a colossal belly that put his belt in constant shade. He pushed out a huge hand for shaking. 'It's good to meet the man at last. I've read your wee pamphlet and we've a deal to talk about, Dessie! Grand to see you again, Elsa, and I see you've brought the wee-uns.'

He slapped his hands together like two slabs of meat and led us all through to the dining room to a long, beautifully set table around which sat twenty-two people.

Dad and our host were trying to hide their political differences behind polite conversation, but you could see the tension in everyone's faces as they chewed slowly and always had the next mouthful ready on the fork.

Dad sat in the middle of the table between two big fellahs and everyone looked at him while he was speaking or listening or eating throughout the meal. He seemed a 'wee man' sitting between those two meat mountains, but he looked battle-hard, determined and difficult, as well.

The host keep battering him with snide comments about his 'wee pamphlet' and some of the 'political inaccuracies'. 'Quite understandable given the calibre of people you've been associating with, Dessie.'

'Some of the people I've been associating with were there on the ground while you were up in your turrets. So let's keep an open mind, shall we?'

'A man with your reputation ought to be careful about who he beds down with.'

Dad busied himself swallowing words as well as mashed potato until he was good and ready. You could see a rage in him that wanted to get out. I felt it rise up through me until my face burned and I wanted to shout out, 'Tell him to get to fuck, the fat bastard!'

Putting my head down quick in case anybody could read my thoughts, I started squashing peas on my plate. I was sick of chasing them with an upside-down fork like Mum had taught me.

Dad pushed his knife and fork together and looked at the fat man. 'We'll take this up later, shall we?'

Then there was a long silence.

You could hear all those mouths chewing and swallowing and the scraping of cutlery on crockery and I looked around the room with its lofty and ornate ceiling, paintings everywhere and the wallpaper that ended with what they called a 'dado rail'.

Then suddenly our host rumbled, 'Aye, it's like they say – every "baah" a sheep makes it misses a bite!'

We all laughed because he'd done the sheep 'baah' so well and it gave us all an excuse to pretend that we were just hungry comrades and not a political pariah and his bastard offspring.

Political movement

Dad left the Communist Party because he said there was nothing for him in it. What he wanted was for someone with 'political know-how' to make sense of what had happened to him. He wanted to use his experience to help bring about a socialist Britain. I thought he was mad.

'You've got more chance of being struck by lightning, Dad.'

'That's what they said to Lenin.'

'That was a totally different situation.'

'Who told you that, your teacher? Who works in an education system that's been designed to produce little gobshites like you to fit into the existing order and perpetuate a social system that doesn't work? You ought to know better.'

'Aye, you're right, Dad. Everything'll change now you've got Vanessa Redgrave behind you.'

'Cheeky bleeder.'

We're driving into town in Dad's 'new' car. It's a fifteen-year-old VW 1600 hatchback and only the driver's door works so I have to climb in through the back. It's not easy to drive. Dad has to twist his foot to straddle the accelerator and the clutch pedal every time he changes gear at low speeds or when it's idling otherwise it stalls. I've asked about lessons but we both know there's no chance. It smells like it rained inside and dried out with all the windows closed.

'So you've actually signed up with the Trots now then, have you?'

'Aye.'

'I bet Mum's chuffed. Being married to the village communist was bad enough, now she's the wife of a raving Trot.'

He laughs and tells me about his training sessions with the

party chairman and other visiting lecturers. It is obvious he is enjoying being 'someone with something to learn' instead of 'the one who took on the system'.

'They tell me what I did right and where I went wrong,' he says. 'That's all I want. How we take these lessons and apply them in order to achieve a socialist democracy – a worker's state.'

'Do you really believe that?'

'What else is there to believe? The working class is sick of answering for the failings of the capitalist system and it wants a viable alternative. Socialism is the only way.'

'Buddhism?'

'Behave yourself!'

Silence

Dinner times were getting so bad at home when Dad was there that I started doing anything to avoid them. I devised a comprehensive timetable of extra-curricular activities to explain why I wouldn't be home till the shouting or the silences were over. Half of them were real, the other half were made up. It was a good system but I didn't really need it. Andy was the only one who showed any interest in where I was at night so it all worked out fine.

By the time I'd get home I'd have swallowed a belly full of mints or chewing gum, and nobody got up off the furniture to do the breath test anyway. I'd pop my head in and see Mum sitting in front of the telly on her rocking chair. I'd say goodnight and go to bed.

The only other increasingly rare variation to this domestic scene was when Dad was home, in which case Mum would be sitting on the sofa and Dad would be sitting in the rocking chair. Because of his condition Dad could make the chair rock without even trying.

We were all getting used to Dad's illness and the doctors and specialists had begun talking about Parkinson's and we all accepted it long before Dad did, without any notion of how devastating it would turn out to be. As a way of dealing with it we reverted to comedy. One time Mum and me were striking a deal about some domestic chore in exchange for some parental allowance and Mum said 'shake on it' and without a moment's thought we both lifted our hands and started quaking.

Dad was in the room at the time and just looked at us quaking and laughing. 'I'm just a figure of fun to you lot,' he said, shaking his head in disbelief, but he was smiling.

It was the last time I saw them smiling together.

Hitting the fan

I came home from school one day, opened the front door and was overwhelmed by the smell of cigarette smoke. Dropping my bag in the doorway I stared in horror and amazement at Diane, who was sitting at the dining table in front of an ashtray full of cigarette butts, wailing in misery with a fag in her mouth.

'What's going on?'

'Dad said ...' Another flood of tears took over.

'Dad said what?'

Andy started explaining but then Dad came through from the lounge and told me that if she wanted to smoke cigarettes he'd teach her how to smoke cigarettes and she wasn't to stop till she'd smoked the whole packet!

I turned on him. 'Who the fuck do you think you are!' Pulling the cigarette out of Diane's mouth, I threw it in the ashtray. 'You stupid bastard.'

'Hey! You're not the head of this family.'

'And neither are you. Go and plan the revolution, you fucking lemon!'

He dropped his tongue over his bottom teeth and swung his fist back then stopped. He lunged at me and caught my chin in his grip. I looked at him for a moment and stepped out of the grip. Then I took Diane, who was still heaving out the tears, and led her upstairs to her bedroom. I sat with her for a while wondering what to do next and then it came to me.

Bounding down the stairs, I picked up the packet with the remaining cigarettes inside and put them in my pocket. Dad had gone back into the lounge and I could hear the rocking chair going over the sound of the telly so I spoke louder than normal.

'I'll have the rest of these fags. It'll save me buying my own down the pub.'

I heard his voice as I slammed the front door and climbed onto my bike.

'Nicky!'

Comfort food

It was important to have a job because then you didn't have to ask for pocket money and explain what you wanted it for, and you could buy your own clothes and not have to wear the embarrassing things your mum bought you.

I got a job at Daffonchio's Fish and Chip Shop in Denbigh. I just walked in there one day after school and asked if there was any work. Mr Daffonchio was a big man with ham-like forearms and a huge belly. He looked as though everyone was getting on his nerves but he said, 'You can start tomorrow.' And I did.

Working in a chip shop was great. You could fry your own supper. Fish and chips was my favourite but sometimes I'd have cheese and onion patties, fishcakes, sausages, chicken breast or even steak and kidney pie. You'd have chips with everything and mushy peas for the health and gravy or curry sauce if you were having the pie.

Mr Daffonchio used to work there as well until I learned how to use the fryer then he didn't come so often except on

Friday and Saturday nights when it got mad busy. His wife used to visit. She was a small, dark-haired woman, who always dressed smart and didn't like talking English. She didn't like talking to staff either, so she mostly just shouted at Mr Daffonchio in Italian. Mrs Daffonchio didn't want her husband to work in the chip shop because it was embarrassing for her.

The manageress was a woman called Doris and she had thin, white hair and glasses. She wore lots of mascara and powder, and blue trousers that clung to her bum. If you had a can of lager she'd be quite sexy. Mr Daffonchio thought Doris was quite sexy as well; sometimes you'd go into the storeroom and they'd both move away from each other and start checking the potato-peeling machine or the order chits stuck to nails on the shelves.

Everybody knew that Mr Daffonchio and Doris were having an affair but you weren't allowed to talk about it. I really liked Doris because she was kind and interested and she liked me. Occasionally I'd touch her bum through her blue trousers that felt like soft plastic and she'd slap my hand and move away.

I loved working in the chip shop but my hair, skin and clothes stank of chip fat all the time and I had massive spots that would never go away.

Binary fission

I was doing well at school and was just a few months from my A-level exams. So when Mum and Dad said they were moving to separate houses in Chester and Buckley I wasn't happy. They had realised, they said, that Dad was never going to get another job so he was going to have to look at alternatives.

Dad and his friend Glyn Cunnah had bought a derelict cottage just around the corner below the abattoir and next to the village shop. The idea was that I would move into that house and do the labouring jobs needed as part of the renovation. This labour in exchange for rent. It meant that I could stay in school.

'I'm not sharing a house with Glyn Cunnah!' I said.

Dad threw his arms up. 'Listen, you gobshite, you'll be living on your own. Glyn's in a wheelchair so he's not going to move into a two-storey dump with no facilities, is he?'

'It's not a dump, is it, Dennis?'

'It's derelict, for Christ's sake, that's the whole point. We renovate it over the year and then we sell it.'

The possibilities for me sunk in pretty quick.

'My own pad!'

'It's a job. It's not a flop house for your mates and girlfriends.'

I was so excited by the idea that it took me a while to realise that Andy was genuinely miserable.

'We're all splitting up,' he said. 'Katy and Christopher are going with Mum. Diane's going to stay at the Steiner Community in Milton Keynes and I'm going with Dad to look after him.'

'What do you mean "look after him"?'

'Well, he's ill, isn't he? He can't live on his own.'

'I suppose so.'

'What about all my friends? What about school?'

'It'll be all right, Andy. I moved here when I was your age. There's plenty of time to make new friends at a new school.'

'I'm not like you.'

'You'll be all right.'

But he wasn't really.

The Welsh wind

It didn't do me any harm when it became known around school that I lived alone.

Added to the wages I got from the chip shop, labouring for Bob Carvel and working the farms, I got £5 a week from Dad for food, but I had to pay the electricity and water out of that. It was a tight budget, but mysterious boxes of food would appear outside the front door from friends' mothers, so I had enough to keep myself in smokes and drink most of the time.

The house was a small one-up, one-down stone-walled construction with low ceilings and doorways. The ground floor was made up of Welsh slate, which gave a beautiful but uneven surface, and the first floor was a mess of blackened pine floorboards roughly nailed into thick oak beams.

Attached to the house was a garage and it was here that

Dad and me put in a bathroom and a second ground-floor room with two extra bedrooms above it. There was a kitchen scullery at the back of the house overlooking a narrow mud footpath with a built-in cupboard under the staircase. The front door opened straight onto the pavement and the 'garden' was a concrete slab for parking a car. This is where Dad left his van most of the time as he could no longer drive all the time because of his illness. It was a decommissioned Post Office van with a 1968 number plate and sliding doors. We drove it with the doors open. I would lean out every now and then, feeling like a paratrooper on an important mission.

I was told that on no account whatsoever was I to drive the van. This warning was so vehemently given that the only times I did drive the van was when I was drunk enough to pluck up the courage.

Man of steel

When he was on form, Dad used to come to the cottage at least a couple of times a week to do some building work. He'd got himself a small car for getting around in and kept the van for fetching and carrying building materials.

When he came at the weekend he'd bring Andy with him. It was always good to see my brother, although he wouldn't stick around for long and he'd be off as soon as he'd brewed a pot of tea to go and visit his old school friends for the day.

Dad was a good builder. He knew a lot about the engineering aspects of most jobs and he could plumb pipes, lay bricks, plaster walls, tile bathrooms, lay screed and chipboard floors, and hang doors and ceilings. I learned a lot from watching and helping.

He seemed calmer and more relaxed now that he was living alone with Andy. He was also seeing a lot of Mum because he was renovating the terraced house that they'd bought for her in Chester.

He was mostly happy with the odd jobs that he'd left me to do about the place during his absences and he never checked the diesel gauge or the milometer on the van so we got on pretty well most of the time. But he was not happy about the abattoir trucks, which were regularly demolishing the low brick wall he had built out in the front.

'What happened there?'

'Meat lorry again.'

'Gobshites.'

The problem was that the road at the front was very narrow with a bus shelter right opposite our house and so the big trucks had to nip over the corner of our property to get up and down the hill that led to the abattoir.

Dad had once spent a whole day building a corner parapet in brick and they'd just driven right over it, crushing it to dust.

'I'll fix them this time.'

'What are you going to do?'

'You'll see.'

We took the van out and went to a local scrap yard where he bought a length of V-shaped steel girder and had them cut it into four sections with a sharp point at the top of each one.

When we got back he told me to dig a hole for foundations where the brick parapet had been. He mixed a load of concrete and filled the hole, then inserted the four steel girders with their sharpened points facing upwards.

'Let's see them drive over that little lot.'

Which they did.

It was a Monday morning during half-term and I was standing on top of a ladder painting a window frame. The window was right on the corner of the house and I was leaning over with a paint brush when I saw the truck coming down from the abattoir. It was an open-topped truck and as it braked at the bottom of the drive I looked down and saw offal swilling backwards and forwards. I wanted to retch. One false move and I'd be in there.

The truck shifted into first gear and drove straight over Dad's steel prongs with a hiss. The outside tyre caved in but the back tyres just rolled over the now flattened steel.

I slowly climbed down the ladder and put my tools away for the day. I thought about phoning Dad to tell him, but he'd find out soon enough anyway.

Roundabout

I'd been in that cottage for a few months when Dad came round one day, not to work but to take me to visit Mum in Chester.

They were separated by now and had been for some time,

pretending they were building up the family finances through small-time property developments because that was the only way Dad could get work to make money. None of us kids really believed this but we all pretended to go along with it. Mum was living with Katy and Christopher in what was supposed to be 'the family home' in Queens Avenue near the train station.

The Queens Avenue house was a two-storey brick terrace under renovation. The result was a scruffy, slightly dirty house with some rooms stripped, plastered and used for storage of building materials, and other rooms newly carpeted and wallpapered by Mum with plaster and brick dust trodden by Dad into the fibres and the fabrics of recently purchased furniture suites and beds. The dust of reconstruction even reached the insides of appliances in the kitchen.

I hadn't seen Mum for months and the last time we had spoken was after I'd asked her for money. I'd used the public call box down the road and she'd said she would see what she could do. I'd called her three weeks later and she'd told me that her bank manager had agreed to a loan of £100 but only if she promised to spend it on a holiday for herself because she was so run down. She was sorry she couldn't help me but promised to mail me a postcard.

Dad was driving and we were waiting to enter a roundabout when he told me casually, 'So your mum and me are getting divorced.'

I stared at him. 'What for? I thought you were building up the family home.'

I had barked it a little too aggressively and Dad looked at me. In that moment I realised that he thought I was going to side with him utterly.

'You know what she's like. I'm up to here with it.'

He started telling me things I knew already and some other things I didn't want to know and I told him to leave me out of it. Somebody banged on their car horn behind us and Dad entered the roundabout at speed and we spent the rest of the journey in an uncomfortable, angry silence.

When we got to Chester he dropped me at the end of the road and said he wasn't coming in. I made my way down the row of redbrick houses. I could see the back of the Mecca Bingo Hall and the chimney stack of the deserted flour mill over the dull grey slates of the rooftops. It was like Coronation Street without the theme tune.

When I got into the chaos that was my mum's home I said hiya to Katy and Christopher, and we all talked about nothing while I strolled through the house past towers of ironing, with the radio and TV filling in all the gaps in a stilted conversation. Mum had that false cheer and she was pretending that it wasn't over with Dad.

She asked me loads of questions about 'the other woman'. I didn't have any answers but I tried to keep it comforting and promising.

The beer talking

The great thing about hay-baling at Foxhall Farm was that you'd get a fiver at the end of every day. I'd go home, have a wash, get some clean clothes on and take my thirst into Denbigh where I'd go from pub to pub with the Denbigh lads or on my own, working my way through town till I was near the Henllan road. At closing time I'd strike off and walk the three miles home.

One night I was walking along, talking to myself and looking up at the black sky through the branches of the trees. The moon was hiding behind silver clouds. The air was thick with fog and I lit a fag to keep me going. Then I just packed in.

I walked off the road through a gateway into a field and I buckled. I sat there for a while and then I felt it all coming and I lay down on my side and wept. Great big gobs of it and I didn't even try to stop it because I knew it wasn't real. I wasn't really sad. It was just the beer.

The Persuader

I had finished my A-levels and was waiting for the results. Dad and me drove to the dump one day in the van. We pulled in with our building rubble and parked near a mountain of similar rubbish. We started unloading from the back of the van. In the distance I heard a diesel engine die, then three men come trotting towards us shouting, 'Hey you! You can't dump that there!'

There was something in their tone that seemed to throw a switch in my dad. He strolled to the cab of our van and pulled out his machete. 'What's that, lads?'

The men stopped in their tracks and started backing away.

I looked at Dad and felt excited but also a bit nervous. I laughed. 'Take it easy, Dad.'

He strode back to the cab and replaced the machete, growling to himself. 'I'm up to here with people telling me what to do.'

I finished unloading the van and when I got back to the cab, I found Dad curled up in a ball on the passenger seat. His face was taut with pain and he muttered almost inaudibly, 'You drive …'

'I haven't got a licence.'

'Drive!'

'Are you all right?'

'Get going.'

I managed to get the thing into reverse and backed up to the exit gates with Dad in the passenger seat destroyed by a total body spasm. It was the worst that I'd seen since his release from prison.

I was swearing at the gearbox and the clutch in a steady stream of colourful language and moaning about the fact that I was going to get pulled over and banned for life. Crunching my way into first gear, I took to the open road with a sideways glance at my father and couldn't believe what I was seeing.

Tears of laughter falling from a frozen grey face.

Moving on

Neil Chinnery got a job as a psychiatric nurse at Denbigh Mental Hospital. Rob Ox and Steve Jones were studying Physics at Manchester. Johnny Fish got married and was having babies. Paul Smith got a job as a forester and moved away. I took a place at Wrexham Art College, despite Mr Daffonchio telling me I had a future in the fast food business, but I couldn't get up most mornings and got kicked out after the first term.

I used to sit for hours staring at the mice eating their way through the vitamin pills in my socks and underpants drawer in the kitchen. I got an air pistol and a catapult but I always missed and the kitchen units were taking a hammering. Then I got a baseball bat and I'd corner and squash them. I'd pin the corpses out on an old dissecting tray of wax I'd kept from Biology, douse them in petrol and watch their eyes pop out and land steaming on the lino. I was drinking plenty but I wasn't eating very well.

One night I had a nosebleed and went downstairs to get some tissue. I heard a rustling in the bin bag and went mad. I got a kitchen knife and stood over the bin bag with blood splashing on my chest, screaming at the bin and stabbing it. When I looked up I saw through the kitchen window somebody running away.

I had to move on but I couldn't.

Then Dad came round with Glyn Cunnah. They said they were selling the house and it was all over.

The last time I saw Henllan was through the window of a bus a little after my eighteenth birthday. I had packed all I could into an old army surplus kit bag and chosen the things that mattered most to me: my filter coffee kit; clothes; some books; tapes and a cassette recorder; art materials; and a very heavy typewriter.

I locked the door of the old cottage and walked over the road to the bus stop and waited for the first bus to take me on the journey to Buckley.

I remember the smell of rough old soiled rubber, discarded sweets, sweat and diesel fumes on the bus, the vibrations at each gear change and the sense of isolation as the journey took me away from my beer-soaked youth.

I'd visited my dad and Andy a few times before and so I knew vaguely how to get to their flat once the last bus had dropped me off on Buckley high street. It was late afternoon. I humped my bags through the winding rows of terraced houses and into the housing estate itself. It was a big estate with two- and three-storey residential buildings well spaced around surreally green lawns. My dad's flat was at the back, with a view of some sorry-looking fields. Rough sods of grass had been stumped up and pitted by the careless hooves of invisible cows and bulls from a nearby farm.

I made my way up the sterile staircase to Dad's first-floor flat and opened the frosted glass door to the back kitchen. There was a stew on the stove and I could hear sounds from the TV bleeding through the serving hatch to the open-plan lounge-dining room. Nobody moved. Dad and Andy were watching TV, Dad in his special Parker Knoll recliner and Andy in the other armchair. The dining table was strewn with newspaper clippings and correspondence that Dad was using as research for his book. I stood in the doorway and accepted their half-hearted greetings. Andy offered me a cup of tea and Dad said my room was all ready for me to move in to.

The idea that they had gone to the effort of making me a room lifted my spirits and I made my way upstairs with my bags to take a look. I opened the door to the room and found boxes of newspaper clippings, an ironing board, piles of washing, a mattress against one wall, sections from a deconstructed bunk bed below the uncurtained window, and all the rubbish that collects despite so many moves to so many new houses that never quite became homes.

I felt heartsore as I stared around and listened to the sarcastic laughter coming from downstairs. I was just another piece of the past that had to be accommodated and I worked hard to suppress the rising feelings of resentment and helplessness. I wanted to leave but where could I go? I dropped my bag and riffled through a side pocket to find my cigarettes. Dad didn't like me smoking but fuck him. I made my way back downstairs.

'I love what you've done with my room – it's great, thanks a lot.'

To my great pleasure that comment seemed to spoil their laughter. Andy pointed to my mug of tea and I took my place on the sofa to watch Googie Withers in *Within These Walls*.

I was to spend the next few months watching that fictional prison series between thousands of hours of dual-play Space Invaders with Andy while Dad was off with one of his girlfriends. I was waiting for my adult life to start.

Endings

Drumnadrochit

Thirty Years On

Shortly after the week I spent with my father in Glan Gerrionedd in 1988, I made my way to Drumnadrochit in search of my birth mother.

I travelled in a camper van and when I arrived in the village that summer's day I asked around the various shops in the village. I finally got the lead I needed at the post office. Yes, they remembered her. Her mother was still alive and living where she always had.

Parking on the road opposite the row of cottages, as close to the exact spot my dad had parked on that snowy night all those years before, I knocked on the door and introduced myself to the old woman who answered.

She was a bent old crone worthy of a children's story and I stepped into the lounge, pushing my way past two decrepit dogs. She was totally unfazed, as if she'd been expecting me. She told me to take a seat and went into the kitchen to put the kettle on. Looking around the room, I couldn't focus on anything. It was just a general assemblage of furniture and ornaments. There was wallpaper everywhere and a busy pattern on the carpet that made your eyes swim.

She told me that my birth mother's sister was staying in a campsite up the road and she'd call her for me, which she did. The woman I spoke to said she remembered me and was full of enthusiasm for a meeting. She'd be over in half an hour.

Putting the phone down, I felt a treacherous anxiety. Did I really want this? I had taken down my birth mother's address during the phone call with my estranged aunty, and that's all I needed. I asked my grandmother if I could possibly trouble her for another cup of tea. She lumbered out of her chair and rattled her way into the back kitchen once more. I took a last look around and headed out of the front door, closing it quietly behind me.

I drove all day until the sun started setting in a wide mountain valley. I passed a campsite set back from the road in a clearing of bramble and heather. Three people were sitting around an open fire. I drove another few miles and pulled into a deserted lay-by, switched off the engine, lights and music, and sat staring into the blackness, listening to the wind and the metal of the engine as it clicked cool.

I felt unsettled and solitary. I had my whole life ahead of me and I didn't know what to do with it. Unable to rest, I drove on till I came across a small grey-stone town and pulled into the car park of a pub where I sat alone on a vinyl chair at a Formica table in a bar room brightly lit by fluorescent tubes. I drank three pints of heavy before turning in for the night.

I travelled as far north as I could go, then all the way down the western edges of the country to Land's End. I rolled out the bed in the camper van every night and thought hard about what to do. In the end I decided to do nothing.

I gave the address of our mother to Andy and Diane, who both made contact. I kept my distance for another fifteen years before writing in 2003.

Her reply arrives at my home in Johannesburg and I inspect the envelope all day. I think that if I read the letter, I won't be able to concentrate on the job I have on my desk at work.

At the end of the day I go home early and see there is only a quarter of an inch of whisky in the bottom of the bottle. I'll need much more than that.

My wife Leila is away for a week in London. After six years of slavish devotion to the raising of our two children, Leila has finally and almost reluctantly taken the opportunity to enjoy a few days of museums and theatre.

My daughter Amelia is playing at a friend's house and I pick up my son Jack and take him with me to the off-licence in the car. I promise an ice cream as an after-trip gift and we wander around the aisles. He is wearing his Spiderman outfit complete with fabric face mask and he has no shoes on his feet so I carry him most of the way.

I waver between Bells, Grants and J&B, and finally settle on the J&B. I'd go for a single malt of the higher order like Laphraoig or Lagavulin but I haven't been paid for a while and funds are low.

I pick up the bottle, which is labelled 'J&B Rare', and admire the copywriting on the label. The 'Rare' appellation is so obviously ridiculed by the fact that there are at least fifty such bottles on the shelf, as well as hundreds of thousands of bottles on all the shelves of all the off-licences in this city alone.

I'm stalling. The letter is in my pocket.

I pick up a bottle of extra virgin olive oil from the supermarket next door as well as ice creams for me and the kids, and head home with Spiderman in the back seat quizzing me about how high tigers can fly and what they eat.

I prepare supper – meat, onions and potatoes for a stew – and set Jack and Amelia up with toys and tasks before I spin the lid of the Scotch and pour a few needy dollops into a tumbler already set up with ice despite my grandfather's advice.

Sitting on the veranda overlooking a riot of exotic blooms in the fading African light, I spark up a cigarette, open the envelope and begin to read.

We lived very boring lives. We had nothing and Aunty Gill was our only visitor. She was angry because Tony had loads of toys and I had none. She told Dad we were the only kids in the area with no toys and so he bought me a milk float. She never knew she would lose her kids.

I was her favourite. I was always asking for water to drink. She asks if I still drink lots of water. I was very caring. She'd get phone calls from Dad's girlfriends, and she'd cry. I would put my arms round her and say,'When I grow up I'll be a doctor and make it all better.' Dad was hardly ever there and she was lonely. She was always just cleaning and washing. Dad left her when she was pregnant with Andy. Two years later she was sent to hospital for a rest and one day Dad visited to tell her he was getting married to a woman called Elsa. She was given electric shock treatment to help her forget. She didn't know what she was supposed to forget. She tried to get her kids back, but with no home, no job and being in a mental hospital she had no chance.

I remember the milk float – everything else is new to me.

A three-frame image appears before my eyes: my father mute and immobile in his bedroom as his latest wife, Pat, mills around in the kitchen, humming a hymn; Elsa alone in her flat across town, patting the furniture, waiting to treat her next hypnotherapy client; and my birth mother, wrapped up warm against the wind, wandering down the garden path to the post box at her front gate, looking to see if I've responded to her letter.

The funeral

Dad died fifteen minutes before midnight on 23 April 2004. I went home for the funeral.

On the early morning tube at Heathrow, people were tired, fierce, valiant, bemused, cocky. Three Scottish businessmen in cheap black suits talked in accents that were now unintelligible to me after so long away. Two gamblers talked about going to Chester for the races. I looked for a familiar face and saw only the spectres of people that could have been friends.

Andy picked me up from the train station in Chester. 'You've put on weight, Nick.'

I asked him how it was.

'I'm not going to lie to you, mate – he didn't go easily. It was a long, horrible, drawn-out death and he struggled to the end.'

I looked out of the car window. Low grey cloud full of spitting rain fell on the black and grey and brightly coloured people scurrying through the Roman streets. I felt removed from everything all over again and the fear of not fitting in crept up.

Dad had lost the ability to swallow weeks before; he was starving and thirsty, and he had developed an infection in his lungs that led to the pneumonia noted as the cause of death on the certificate.

I visited Pat, his widow, before spending most of the evening with Andy who gave me his unsentimental version of the death: 'He drowned on his own spit.'

Andy always used to say, 'Don't go to that pub; it's full of old fogeys.' Now he said, 'Don't go in that pub; it's full of kids.' We've been drinking together for over twenty years – through a whole generation.

We drank in the Union Vaults that night, a real and uncompromising pub in a back street, and talked about what we would each like to say at the funeral if we were to be given the chance. Andy mentioned a letter Dad had written to Bert Ramelson from Stafford prison in February 1974. He quoted verbatim: "'I look forward to my day of release so that I can rejoin the struggle, not with a feeling of bitterness or revenge but with a strengthened resolve to help bring about a Socialist Britain." And that's why they couldn't let him out, isn't it? When the prison censors and the Home Office read that they decided there was no chance.'

It was cited as 'the family's wishes' that the funeral be non-political in nature and so most of the men and women who wanted to mark the end of a life spent in the struggle for a better world were asked not to make speeches.

The service was conducted by a preacher from the Pentecostal Church to which Pat belonged. Pat had told me proudly one day that my father had also joined the same church a few years ago. I remember asking Dad about this later when Pat was out of the room and he raised his eyebrows and set his mouth in that hyphen of a smile for me to interpret.

I was surprised and disappointed when I felt that the preacher turned the funeral of my father into a marketing opportunity. It was difficult to listen to the relentless sermonising as he seemed to me to almost scrub out my father's political life and rewrite his death as the ultimate religious epiphany. It was impossible for me to look at the man delivering what felt like a final betrayal and it took every effort for me to maintain my own silence.

Apart from an all too brief but poignant memorial by Ricky Tomlinson, I felt I was mourning the passing of a happy-clapping stranger who had finally attained his greatest earthly wish – to melt into the arms of the Lord.

There were lots of people at the wake afterwards and even though no stage had been prepared there was no stopping the testimonies of my father's life and influence being exchanged by those who knew him as a fighter.

I spent the next few days visiting childhood haunts, and when I got back to Chester I asked Pat what was planned for the ashes. She was a little flustered as she told me that they had already been scattered in the Garden of Remembrance by one of the crematorium employees. 'If you'd been here you could have made other arrangements, Nick, but it was all so difficult to know what to do.'

I never watched him die. I never saw him dead. I never heard his due eulogies. I never scattered his ashes.

Pat, who had looked after Dad through the last and most difficult fifteen years of his life, died suddenly and shockingly from a brain haemorrhage after a fall just four weeks after Dad's funeral.

I was back in Johannesburg and couldn't go to Pat's funeral so it was up to her sons and Andy to empty the flat in which they'd lived together.

I don't know what happened to Dad's belongings – his turtleneck sweaters, his training pants, his shirts, his prison notebooks. I got his old brown leather wallet from the basement after the funeral, empty when I opened it but for three Silver Jubilee Celebration stamps from 1977.

As I look at it now I think it's a strange privilege to be a parent. It's an easy privilege to abuse. There is so much expectation and adoration and yet it's only a matter of time before those positive reflections wane in the light of unexpected events and inevitable growth.

For some this disillusion comes early in the wake of physical and mental abuse from broken people expressing their own weaknesses on their young. For others it comes later, first with adolescence and its necessary rebellions, and later with a more mature assessment of the parent's limitations. And there is a Peter Pan syndrome whereby the child wants to cling to the formative images of parental greatness and invulnerability for as long as possible and this itself fuels an anger at their passing.

Every parent is an anecdote waiting to be told. At some point, for some years, or perhaps only on one fine and social evening, those stalwart and unpredictable icons of the familial past will become conversational currency to be exchanged among relative strangers.

All one can wish for is that the bulk of those stories will be good ones, and that new stories will continue be made and told with enthusiasm.

Eulogy

Here lies an ordinary man.

A man made great by his principled reactions to extraordinary
  circumstances.

A man who lived by what he believed in.

A man who was ultimately destroyed for those beliefs.

A man I am proud to call my father, and the grandfather of my
  children.

See you, Dad.

Last words

I'll leave the last word to Dad. His speech in court, delivered after the verdict, reflects a spirit and a belief that kept him going over the thirty years of what Ricky Tomlinson called his 'life sentence':

'It has been said in this court that this trial had nothing to do with politics. Among the ten million trade unionists in this country I doubt if you will find one who would agree with that statement. It is a fact of life – entirely due to Acts of Parliament – that every strike which takes place is regarded as a political act. It therefore follows that every act taken in furtherance of an industrial dispute also becomes a political act.

'There are even those who describe as a challenge to the law of the land, the action of men who decide not to work beyond the agreed number of hours in the working week and who ban overtime.

'This is something not of the making of the trade unions. Politically motivated interference by governments acting on behalf of and under political pressure from employers, now means that no trade unionist can enter freely into negotiations with employers.

'They cannot withdraw their labour – the only thing they possess as a bargaining lever – without being accused of setting out to wreck the economy, of challenging the law.

'The building employers, by their contempt of the laws governing safety regulations, are guilty of causing the deaths and maiming of workers – yet they are not dealt with by the courts.

'Mr Bumble said, "The law is an ass." If he were here now he might draw the conclusion that the law is quite clearly the instrument of the state to be used in the interests of a tiny minority against the majority.

'It is biased, it is class law, and nowhere has that been demonstrated more than in this trial. The very nature of the charges, the delving into ancient Acts of Parliament to dredge up "conspiracy" shows this to be so.

'Was there a conspiracy? Yes, there was, but not by the pickets. The conspiracy began when the miners gave the government a good hiding last year, and I hope they do the same again. It developed when the government was forced to perform legal gymnastics to get five dockers out of prison after having only just put them there. The conspiracy was one between the Home Secretary, the employers and the police. It was not done with a nod or a wink. It was conceived after pressure from Tory MPs who demanded changes in picketing laws.

'There is a very good reason why no police witness said here that he had seen any evidence of conspiracy, unlawful assembly or affray. The question was hovering over the case from the very first day: Why no arrests on the sixth of September? That would have led to even more important questions: When was the decision to proceed taken? Where did it come from? What instructions were issued to the police, and by whom? There was your conspiracy.

'I am innocent of the charges and I will appeal. But there will be a more important appeal made to the entire trade union movement from this moment on. Nobody here must think they can walk away from this court and forget what has happened here. Villains or victims, we are all part of something much bigger than this trial.

'The working-class movement cannot allow this verdict to go unchallenged. It is yet one more step along the road to fascism and I would remind you: the greatest heroes in Nazi Germany were those who challenged the law when it was used as a political weapon by a government acting for a minority of greedy, evil men.'

Des Warren
Shrewsbury Picket, 1973